T0107810

THE PAIN OF DESTINY
Vow to Survive

Brandon O. Severs Sr.

iUniverse, Inc.
Bloomington

The Pain of Destiny
Vow to Survive

Copyright © 2012 Brandon O. Severs Sr.

iUniverse books may be ordered through booksellers or by contacting:

iUniverse
1663 Liberty Drive
Bloomington, IN 47403
www.iuniverse.com
1-800-Authors (1-800-288-4677)

ISBN: 978-1-4697-6123-7 (sc)
ISBN: 978-1-4697-6124-4 (hc)
ISBN: 978-1-4697-6125-1 (e)

Library of Congress Control Number: 2012901942

Printed in the United States of America

iUniverse rev. date: 1/30/2012

This book is dedicated to my sunshine, Shadora.

What if the promise inside of you
could change the world?

Before I formed thee in the belly I knew thee...

—Jeremiah 1:5

CONTENTS

FORWARD

Being different is not a bad thing. It's the thing that makes us an individual and allows us to become who we are. It is the thing that identifies us from everyone else. Struggles make us into who we are. Like the earthly caterpillar that builds the cocoon to await its transformation, who struggles and presses to free itself from its captivity and imprisonment to develop into a beautiful and heavenly butterfly. Struggling is to mold us into who we are to be. It makes us push and strive to become what God would have us be. Disappointments cause us to work to change our present situations and failures into success. Experiences help to identify our needs. Pain is to help us recognize a problem and seek to identify the cause in order to change the situation. God allows us to experience these emotions, and we feel that he has dealt us a dirty blow. In life, sometimes we feel that He has forsaken us, but the Bible promises that He will never leave us nor forsake us. He will always be there to see us through difficult situations and help us make the right decisions, whether we choose them or not. He will always be beside us.

I applaud the author for his candid expressions. It takes great courage to share the personal and intimate details of one's life. There are many young people, as well as older individuals, struggling with the same challenges of molestation, mental and physical abuse, and sexual promiscuity. They are suffering in silence, feeling fear, rejection, guilt, and shame. They are too fearful to reach out for help, not knowing who to turn to.

Through your book, you have given people the hope of knowing that no matter what they go through in their life, they are able to conquer all situations. They may let themselves down, but as long as they pursue Jesus Christ, they can persist through their failures until they achieve their God-given success inside them. I pray the testimony in this book you have presented will help others to find hope in Christ Jesus, as you have, and to search for the gift that lies within them and to not abort their dreams and visions.

INTRODUCTION

Life can be an exciting adventure one day and a nightmare the next.

Why is it that some people seem to be destined for greatness, while others have to struggle to attain life's basic necessities? If God is no respecter of person, why is life so difficult for some and seemingly a walk in the park for others? Why is it that criminals can maim and kill and then walk free while the innocent must struggle to remain alive because of the actions of another? What is God's definition of grace and mercy? Is it the same as ours?

I ask these questions because of the life that I now live. It seems I often strived for greatness but settled for mediocrity, as if I were against myself rather than being successful, and I seemingly enjoyed and often seemed destined for self-destruction. Ever since I was a child, I felt different from other children. I was never really able to fit into a crowd or go along with the norm or status quo. I'm a good person. Why do bad things always happen to me? I am kind to people and animals; I don't bother anyone. People who do bad things always seem to live the best lives. Life really isn't fair. Or so I thought.

I was shot during a home invasion. Someone I thought was a very good friend set me up after I let him spend the night at my home. My pregnant wife was fine but had to take on the tasks of taking care of me and our child; seeing about her mother, who was in a nursing home; working a full-time job; and running a household by herself. Getting shot had to be one of the most character-building events in my life. I learned much about myself, my family, my friends, and, most of all, God.

Chapter 1

HOW IT ALL BEGAN

I have always aspired for greatness; however, most times I was mediocre and I procrastinated, which for me seemed to be second nature. I have always attained popularity because of organizations that I was a part of or quirks in my personality. I was raised in a large family, and I am the youngest of five siblings. I have one younger sister, with whom I share the same father. I was born to a single mother. My mother, bar none, is the strongest woman I knew, when it pertained to faith and perseverance. My mother is the model of self-sacrifice, whose mission in life was to ensure the health, well-being, and happiness of myself and my siblings, most times putting her needs and wants secondary. For years, my mother, receiving no help from the fathers of her children, found herself raising all of them by herself. In the 1980s, my mother and all five of us children found ourselves homeless. We were never homeless to the point of living on the streets; however, we resided in an abandoned crack house. There were times when the crack addicts would come in the house through the front door and we would hurry out the back door. My mother always prayed about everything. Though she made mistakes along her path, she always believed in God and the power of prayer. Later she would have a chance encounter with a gentleman at a grocery store, and despite her lack of interest in him, he would see the need for a father in our lives and would later become my stepfather. My two older siblings called him by his first name. They were already in their teens. However, my other two siblings, who were closer in age to me, and I called him Daddy.

Earl (Daddy) is the epitome of a man. It wasn't just because of his sex but because he was a real man when it came to his life with his new family He never treated any of my mom's kids as his stepchildren. Even though he was financially well-off, owning his own business and working a nine-to-five and endless side jobs, he downgraded his lifestyle to make sure that we had the best that he could afford. The shopping sprees and brand-name labels that he showered us with paled in comparison to the life lessons he taught us, especially my older brother and I. He taught us the meaning of being a real man and caring for a family by the example he led with his life. No matter what it was in life, he saw to it that we had it. He was a lot older than my mother, and wisdom rested on his shoulders, and even though we didn't want to always hear nor had confidence in what he had to say, we respected him.

My father, Charles "Chop-Chop," was a heroin-addicted drug dealer and abuser up until the day he died. His entire life was spent in and out of jail and the penitentiary. Even though I was his only male child and I'm the spitting image of him, he never believed I was his child, an opinion that was heavily influenced by his mother, who also shared this same belief. It was rare that he would spend time with me. He thought it was something really wonderful to act like a Santa Claus of sorts when it came to other children by giving them what they wanted because he loved the praise he would receive for doing things for them. However, he would never do anything for me. I asked him one day, "Why are you never there for me?" He replied, "Because you got a good momma."

Over my entire life I received a gift of one hundred dollars in cash and, a few years later, a toy robot, which was nothing for him. He began to like me even less the day he asked me what I wanted to be when I grew up and I replied, "A police officer!" Although he acted most of the time as if I didn't exist and I had a great dad at home, I loved my father and wanted him to at least act as if he liked or even loved me. What I wanted most from my father was love and some time. I looked up to my father, and I wanted to be just like him. I even asked him if I could sell drugs for him, and he was willing to allow it. I never followed through with selling drugs for him, though he was so proud of me—all the while never considering the consequences. I really don't think people realize how much it hurts a child to know a parent is alive, known of, or seen but remains absent from a child's life. When my father died, he was penniless. I still loved him and footed the bill for all but four hundred dollars of his funeral. I could not afford to have him buried, so he was cremated. I kept his ashes because, even though he was not living and was now cremated, I finally had my dad.

The earliest memory that I have of my childhood was when I was three years old. My mother and my other four siblings and I relocated to Tucson, Arizona, where my mother was born and raised. We lived in the home of my grandmother, along with my aunt and three of her sons. As to be expected, the home was always filled with people, whether it is family or friends of my grandmother coming to visit and saying their final good-byes, as cancer was spreading through her body and she was dying. A cousin of mine, who was about seventeen years old, began to sneak me into the bathroom. There, my innocence as a child was lost. In that place, which was used for cleaning and grooming, I was made to feel dirty. He made me perform unspeakable acts of oral sex on him, making it plain that no one could ever know of the game that we played. It was our secret not to be shared with anyone, or I would be in trouble, so I was fearfully persuaded to keep my silence, not knowing what danger I would face if I ever broke it. In addition, another family member, who was just a few years older than I, was also being forced to play this game.

I carried this horrible secret for a while. I suppressed it, but after about twelve years, I finally found the courage to expose the heinous acts of this monster. I had come to a point in my life where I no longer wanted to carry the baggage that I was forced to. I will never forget that night. It was New Year's Eve of 1994.I was a freshman in high school. My mother was in her room resting, and with tears in my eyes,

I said, "Momma, I got to tell you something." As with any mother who has a relationship with her child, she could immediately sense that something was seriously wrong. Trying to be as strong as she could, she replied, "What's the matter?" So at this point I could no longer hold back the tears, and I said to her, "Momma, if I tell you something, you have to promise that you won't be mad." Even though I knew I was completely safe, I guess I said this because I was getting ready to expose something that I was promised would cause me grave danger. To some extent I still believed it and I was terrified. I began to give an account of what was done to me in vivid detail, as if it were yesterday. I let her know the acts that my cousin had been making me do to him sexually. After she consoled me and was crying herself, brokenhearted and feeling like the protection she gave me somehow wasn't sufficient, she assured me I was safe and that no one was going to hurt me or anyone else for that matter. Shortly thereafter, my mother called my sister and my brother into the room and told them what had happened to me and asked them if this had happened to either one of them, also giving them the same assurance she had given me. I guess this is what gave another family member the courage to expose what he had been doing to them. My mother notified her sister, my cousin's mother, and she talked to him, and that was it. Nothing else was ever done to avenge us; no authorities were notified or anything. The only thing I can attribute to that was we didn't have the awareness that we have today about child molestation.

When I was eighteen, I took a trip to Bakersfield to visit family, and I met up with the cousin who had violated me sexually. He gave me what he considered an apology, saying he was sorry if the *game* that we used to play when we were younger had hurt me and that I shouldn't forget that I had wanted to play the *game* also. But I hadn't wanted to do that. I was only three years old. I had no idea what I was doing, but I knew it wasn't right. It baffles my mind even to this day how utterly sick and morbid a person's mind can be. The *game* was never consensual. For Christ's sake, I was only a toddler.

This had such a tremendous impact on my life, from being extremely promiscuous at an early age to dealing with major homosexual thoughts, mannerisms, and extreme sexual desires even before puberty. I often wonder what thoughts could have been in my mind had this never happened. What ingenious or witty things could I have come up with had I not been bombarded with this mess? Why didn't I have anybody in my life who thought I was worth fighting for to the extent of him being legally prosecuted, which he deserved? Wasn't I worth it?

How could a life like this ever amount to anything? All throughout my adolescence and adult life, I dealt with dysfunctional relationships that I now attribute to what happened in the past—things that were major life-altering distractions teamed with improper self-destructive behaviors. Behaviors that at times threatened my freedom and my life. There have been three major relationships in my life that have helped shape how I handle relationships. A lot of things that transpired I am not proud of. As I look back, there were so many things that I could have done better in my life.

Hindsight is always twenty-twenty. Anytime we think of mistakes that have been made, especially considering others, we always get a case of the "should have, would have, could haves," rarely considering the variables that caused a particular action. I can plainly see how someone else would have handled things, especially concerning my biggest cheerleader and enemy—me. The mistakes of the past are learning experiences for the future. If applied properly, they can lead and guide you to a future with far less regrets.

I love the Lord. I never wanted the lifestyles of a lot of my peers. In high school I joined a junior fraternity, and because of the popularity that followed, I was exposed to so much. The slang term that describes it best would be that I was "turned out." When you "go online" (which is the probation period, if you will, to becoming a member of a fraternity) for membership in a junior fraternity club, you are given a nickname. Mine was given because of my size and personality. I was called Reverend Too Big, and by the time I crossed over or became a member of the club, I was given another nickname based on the way I was presently, and I was called Reverend Too Nasty." Though this name screamed "hypocrite," I was confused; and though I was extremely sexually active, I was still looked to by my peers for spiritual advice, guidance, and prayer.

Chapter 2

DYSFUNCTION AND DATING

First there was Olivia. Olivia was something else. She appeared to be a quiet little schoolgirl. I met her at a party while I was in high school. She was a year and a half younger than I was. Although we couldn't see each other often because we went to different schools, she ran track and, one day, I went to one of her track meets. After she completed her event, she came to the bleachers, where I was sitting, and we talked for a short while. Physically I was not the person she thought I was the night we met because later on that night she broke up with me because I was not "cute" to her anymore. I was crushed. Eventually we got back together. Her mother worked two jobs, which left her and her little sister home with no supervision. This gave us freedom to do whatever we wanted to do. I was still a virgin, and eventually we began to have sex, rarely ever using a condom. Now, even though she was younger than I was, she was far more experienced in sexual matters. Old folks would say she was fast.

Now, I was being raised in what I thought was a strict Christian home. My mother was serious about us keeping ourselves pure until marriage. She emphasized that we were absolutely not to partake in premarital sex, even though my stepfather lived with us for years and they weren't married. My mother was always praying, and God seemed to always answer her prayers. As a scare tactic, she told my older brother and me that she prayed and asked God to let our penises get crooked if we had premarital sex. We were so afraid of that happening, and it worked for a while; but after we found out that it was a bogus attempt to keep us from having sex before marriage, we went wild.

Olivia made me work hard to get her, and soon the tables were turned, and I began to show a lack of interest. Still intrigued by the fact that we were having sex, we began to have sex on an almost-daily basis. One day I got a phone call from her that would change my life forever. Olivia was on the other end, terrified; and with her voice cracking, she told me her period was late. Every day when we would talk on the phone, the first thing I would say was "Did your period come?" and she would reluctantly reply, "No." This went on for months. I was not ready to be a father, and she definitely was not ready to be a mother. That's when we came to the conclusion that she needed to have an abortion. I was too afraid of what people might say, and I definitely didn't want to tell my mom and dad; after all, neither one of my parents knew I was sexually active. I had the reputation of a church boy, so something like this would surely damage the facade I was keeping up.

I hate how I handled that whole situation. I wish now that I let her have my baby, but I had doubts because she was never really faithful, and most of all I was scared. I am ashamed to even tell the next part of this story, which to this day no one really knows. I let Olivia know that I could not take the blame for this and that she would have to handle this on her own. I told her to tell her mother that while she was at a party one night, she met a guy who was visiting from out of state and who was in college; they hooked up and had a one-night stand, and now her period was about three months late. She also had tried to find him and couldn't. I told her to tell her mother that she wanted to have a pregnancy test, and if she was pregnant, she wanted to have an abortion.

Her mother was devastated, and shortly thereafter, Olivia had the abortion. Olivia said that she nearly backed out of doing it because as she was lying on the table she could feel the baby moving around in her stomach, something that she had never felt up until that moment. She had never felt the baby do anything until that day. Afterward, I begged her to forgive me, and she did, and then I had to forgive myself, and most of all, I had to ask God to forgive me. It still hurts even to this day. She was four months pregnant. As time went on, we began to date other people, but we stayed in contact for no other reason than to have sex. Even after all that, we still did not use a condom. It is so strange, but you can know to do better and still not. We would sporadically try an exclusive relationship, but it was never right.

In the midst of a new school year, I met another girl, who would prove to be a force to be reckoned with. Secondly there was Danielle. I could have titled an entire chapter after her. The things that Danielle and I caused for ourselves and what we went through dwarfed my prior woes. She and I met in school and got into a relationship, and it was not long until we were in the sheets. Danielle was a freshman, and I was a senior in high school. At seventeen, I should have known better. She was fourteen, but to me she had the body of a grown woman. I'm not making an excuse—I am trying to paint a picture. She was gorgeous. I would later find myself comparing every other girl I have ever been with to her. Danielle had a hold on me, which I didn't know if I could ever break free from. I know love can make you do some crazy things; now couple that with teenage hormones. The things I accepted and did while we were together even surprised me.

We grew up right around the corner from each other and had never met. Her looks really made it intimidating for me to try and talk to her, so I had my cousin introduce us. In the beginning she lied about her age, and by the time I found it out, we were already together. Once again I found myself playing a game of cat and mouse. And once again the chase was seemingly worth it. We did any and everything we wanted to do whenever and wherever we wanted to as long as her parents didn't know anything about it. Things didn't start out overwhelming; they were very subtle in the beginning, as with many things in life that we end up succumbing to and oftentimes become overtaken by. Things started off with us just kissing, and I really couldn't French kiss. Olivia and I never did, but Danielle liked to, and the very first time Danielle and I kissed was horrible. I asked

Olivia if she knew how to French kiss and if she would teach me. She didn't suspect a thing because I told her I wanted to learn for her; after all, we were dating, and she had no idea about Danielle and that I wanted to learn this for Danielle, so she taught me. Danielle and I, having no inhibitions, began to have foreplay on the school bus during the ride home. I don't know how we were never caught. I wish now that things would have remained as simple as just a kiss. Now all the while I was afraid to talk to her and was intimidated by her beauty, she was equally intimidated by me because she was a virgin, and she thought that if she told me this, I would no longer like her. During one of our episodes on the school bus, I found out that she was a virgin; however, she couldn't have been more wrong. The fact that she was a virgin made me like her even more.

One year during spring break, I began to go over to her house while her parents weren't home. Essentially, that was the beginning of the travesty that we would call a relationship. Over the spring break the promises that she had made to her father of remaining pure until she was married were now broken. We thought we were in love; hormones can often give this illusion. Danielle's parents didn't allow her to date, so consequently, all of our dealings were behind their backs until one day during summer break while she was at her cousin's house. Her parents, having suspicions that something was awry with their daughter, searched her bedroom. The innocence of their child was forever lost the moment they stumbled upon one of the sexually explicit love letters that she and I would write each other. Her parents were not only hurt but they were also livid. After finding out whom I was and that I was eighteen years old, her mother immediately wanted to call the authorities and have me arrested for statutory rape. Her father, however, was a little more levelheaded and old fashioned, and he decided to call my parents and have a meeting with me, my parents, Danielle, and the both of them.

I was humiliated as my mother read the sexually explicit letter I had written and, at the same time, was extremely grateful that they didn't call the police and have me arrested. The lesson was not learned because our devious ways continued. She didn't have much to lose. I was the one risking going to jail, so even though we were dating, she began to sneak around with other boys behind my back.

I was very popular in high school, and I kept in touch with underclassmen that I had developed friendships with. One of these friends told me about one of the guys that she was sneaking around with because they were getting pretty serious. I didn't go to college right out of high school; I got a job delivering furniture. One morning while at work, I decided that after I left the warehouse loading my truck, I was going to drive up to her school, find this boy, and beat him down for messing around with my girl. When I arrived at the school, none of the faculty said anything to me as I searched through the school for this boy. In retrospect, how incredibly stupid could I have been. I had my company's truck loaded down with expensive furniture. I was at a school looking for a minor boy so I could fight him for messing around with a girl who was cheating on me and whose parents just afforded me the mercy of not throwing me in jail.

I turned back to Olivia at this point. Danielle and I were pretty much done messing around, and even though she didn't know it, Danielle could have had my undivided attention. I bounced back and forth between the both of them as time went on. I changed jobs and was making pretty good money, and I moved into my own apartment. Soon thereafter, I found out that Danielle was pregnant and by me. Even though I could financially afford a child, I still had the same cowardly views, not wanting to accept responsibility for my actions. We went and had an abortion. I still remember standing in the lobby of the abortion clinic, holding the ultrasound picture. With tears in my eyes, I said to myself, "Wow, she looks just like me," even though what I was looking at was just a speck on a piece of paper. I was in the waiting room for what seemed like hours when really it was only thirty minutes. When it was all over, we got in my car and went out to lunch. It seemed to be no big deal. It was as if we had gone to the doctor for a checkup. I remember going into the bathroom at the restaurant. I locked the door on the stall and began weeping uncontrollably. A while later, I gathered myself together, came back to the table, ate my lunch, and took her back home.

At this point I was using abortion as a form of birth control. No one really talks about the emotional scars that men have when this happens. Abortion seems like a simple remedy to an otherwise bad situation, but it affects many. I have often wondered about the contributions that the child we murdered could have made in this world. I didn't look at what we were doing with the severity that I thought I had.

Even though we said we were in love, Danielle still continued to see other guys behind my back, and I was just as bad because I still had the occasional romp with Olivia, among many other girls. We still held on to the lie that we were together.

I was nineteen when I moved out of my parents' house; as a matter of fact, it was my nineteenth birthday. This gave Danielle a place to sneak off to. Neither I nor my siblings would have dared have sex in my parents' house. Growing up, we couldn't even have company upstairs, let alone in our bedrooms. One day while out running errands, I met up with the neighborhood "fun girl." She knew what I wanted, and she wanted me, so she was more than willing. She thought that by having sex with me, I would want to have a relationship with her, which couldn't have been further from the truth; but I was not about to tell her any different. She thought that I was different from all the other guys in the neighborhood because I was so unlike everyone who was gangbanging. To some extent, I was. My grandfather had a saying: "A hard penis doesn't have a conscience." If I needed to have her think that I was going to be in a relationship with her to get what I wanted, I was more than willing. This was going to be an easy conquest. I invited her up to my apartment, and we slept together, and as usual, I didn't use any protection.

The old saying goes, "God protects babies and fools," and I was a little of both. I felt like a big man. I was steadily sleeping with three different girls whenever I wanted to, and none of them knew what was going on. Pride comes before a fall, and believes me, I fell hard—flat on my face. In one day, I got phone calls from all of them, and each said the exact same thing. "Brandon, my period is late!" I thought I literally was going to lose my mind. I could not fathom how this was happening to me—all of them at the exact same time. How in the world was this happening to me? I wanted to go away. I wanted to hide and die—anything—than face this situation head-on.

I did the only thing I knew to do when faced with a situation that is beyond my control: I prayed. I didn't just say a few prayers and hope for the best. I shut myself up in my bedroom for two days, and I cried out to God. I begged him to forgive me for the sin of fornication and pled to him for his mercy and to not let any of these girls be pregnant. I promised I would turn from my sinful ways and abstain from premarital sex if he would just let this not be so. God doesn't operate on the barter system. Grace and mercy made a grand entrance in my life the next few days because all of the girls got their periods. The sighs of relief could be heard 'round the world.

For a while I kept my promise to the Lord, and I abstained from sex. Danielle and I became as exclusive as we could while still keeping our relationship from her parents. We would meet up when we could and talk on the phone when it was possible, and that was fine with us. We would make the most of our time together. We made it work. We both were raised in the church, and we knew what was required of us, and we should have stopped communicating like her parents and the law demanded, but we didn't. Searching to ease our guilty consciences, we began to pray and read the Bible together. Danielle and I were not having sex anymore with each other or anyone for that matter.

One day while I was attending an awards ceremony at my niece's elementary school, which was around the corner from our houses, Danielle walked up to the school to see me. I walked her back home when it was over. It was extremely hot, and it was the middle of the day when we arrived at her home. Of course her parents weren't there, so she invited me in. She fixed us both some ice water, and we sat in a room with the air-conditioning on. She said that she was not cooling off fast enough and took off her dress. There she stood in a black lace bra-and-panty set, and my hormones couldn't handle this abstinence any longer. We fell right back into the same trap that we tried hard to come out of. Eventually with the both of us falling back into our old habits, we figured it was time to start seeing other people; however, it was mutually agreed that we would stay in the background for each other.

I went on to pursue my comedy career, and I had an opportunity to be on a comedy show, which meant relocating to Atlanta, Georgia. Danielle persuaded me not to do it because she wanted to be back together. She would be graduating and going off to college soon, and it wouldn't matter that her parents didn't approve of us being together. Danielle came up with the plan that I could work and support us while she was in college, and when she graduated, she would support us and I could pursue my career full-time. How foolish I was to believe her. I passed on the opportunity to go to Atlanta. I guess I thought that by her telling me this, we were back together, which was not so because she began to date everyone who showed her any interest. I heard more stories from friends and mutual acquaintances about the guys she was dating.

She had a part-time job at a local department store, and on her lunch break, she would call me up there and we would have sex in my car. One day she called to tell me she was going on a break and to not to wait for her in the parking lot but rather to meet her inside the store because she had something to tell me. When I arrived, I sat in the parking lot for a while because I just knew she was going to tell me that she was pregnant. After sitting in my car with a million thoughts racing swiftly through my mind, I finally mustered up the courage to face my impending fate. When I finally approached her, she was acting very distant and not at all happy to see me, which was not unusual because she often had mood swings. She then said, "Brandon, we are through—forever this time and I mean it. I can't do this anymore. This is just too much. My parents have disapproved of this from the beginning." She said that she was tired of sneaking around. "My parents don't want me dating you or anyone for that matter, and I have found someone new." She said that she had found someone who understood her in a way that I never could and that she was in love, and she needed me to step aside because the only way they could be together was if I were to step away completely. Her new interest knew me and a lot about me and could tell me of events that went on in my life. Intimate details of my life, that no one could have known about, unless they were close to me. My mind immediately began to wonder who this could be. She said even though I had never met this person, they didn't particularly care for me, as I had caused much opposition in their life. As a matter of fact, I interfered in a relationship that this new person she'd found wanted prior to Danielle. This new person thought that they could have had it all with their ex-lover that I interfered with, but after person's ex had an abortion, things were just never the same between them. This person hated me, even though I had, as far as I knew, never laid eyes on this person. To my surprise, as a small world would have it, the new person knew me because she used to be with Olivia. Her new person was a girl and was Olivia's ex-girlfriend.

I was floored. I was angry and embarrassed. I began to question my manhood. I thought maybe I was turning these girls gay. The relationship between the two of them apparently didn't last too long because shortly thereafter I took Danielle back into my life. We weren't back together, but we were back in the sheets every chance we got. We celebrated Valentine's Day at my apartment that year. I had the lights turned down low and some very sensual music playing in the background. I lined a path from my bedroom door to my Roman bathtub with rose petals, where I had a hot-milk-and-honey bubble bath awaiting her. I slowly undressed her and carried her to the bathtub; after bathing her, I wrapped her in a towel, picked her up in my arms, and carried her to the bed, where I massaged her body with lotion and we made what I thought was love.

Needless to say, that day she became pregnant. This time when she told me, I felt differently about it. I actually wanted the baby. No amount of talking was enough to convince her to keep our baby. She and one of her friends went to a clinic, and she had yet another abortion. Here I was, barely twenty years old, and every child that I have ever fathered was now aborted. One would think that would be enough, but like I said before, this girl had a hold on me. Danielle had gone off to make a life for herself, and her plans no longer included me. She went away to pursue her career, and I no longer heard from her except for the occasional letter in the mail.

For the first time in my life, I was focusing on me. I joined a church, and now I had become a Christian comedian. I was about to venture off into a new realm that I simply was not prepared for. I had a friend named Dave. We met in high school, and we were complete opposites; however, we became inseparable, or so I thought. Dave was highly intelligent, and he began working for a company where he rapidly advanced in. Eventually his job transferred him to another state. He was there for about six months, and he asked me to move there with him because he had no family there. I was not getting the big break I needed in Las Vegas, so I decided to give it a shot. Shortly before I packed my bags to leave, I got a phone call from— guess who—Danielle. She was living in a city a few miles from where Dave was now living. Before I moved out there, I met another girl, Shadora. To my surprise she was only seventeen, and we could not do anything as far as a relationship. Danielle and I had a history, and I was moving to the same state she was in, so why not give it a try? We were both a little older and wiser; perhaps things would be better. Danielle and I discussed getting back together again and maybe even getting married, but in the back of my mind was this girl I had just met before I left home, Shadora. Even though she was way younger than I was, there was something drawing me to her. Danielle had no idea what she wanted even after all these years. It was as if she did not want me, but she did not want anybody else to have me.

Danielle had a friend whom she met when she moved away. She would often speak of her and even went as far as calling her a sister. Danielle said she and this girl were so close because when things went on in either of their lives they were there for each other. One night I slept over at Danielle's apartment, and when she got up to go to work, I stayed there and I cleaned her house. I did a little snooping, and I must say that when you go looking for something, don't be upset when you find it. While cleaning I came across some photographs in a drawer turned upside down, and I knew they were like that for a reason. I found pictures of Danielle naked, which was not too alarming because I had taken pictures of her like that before; but as I looked further through these pictures, I saw naked photos of a girl I did not know, who was also naked. After confessing what I did to Danielle and having a heated argument, I found out it was the girl she called her sister, and she angrily later confessed that they were ex-lovers. She let me know that they were no longer in a relationship, but they still had ties that bind, and she was not willing to eliminate her from her life. When I gave her the ultimatum of her or me, she chose her.

I finally made the decision to make a clean break, never looking back, and it was probably the hardest thing that I have done. As logical, thinking people, no one would go and play hopscotch on the freeway or run sharp blades across our skin because we know it will cause pain, but we will subject our emotions to danger even when we know that danger is lurking. I was still living in that town, and I was frantically searching for a job. One day, Dave suggested we go get some Chinese. While we were having dinner, he told me that he wanted me to leave his home. While I was praying one night, he asked to stop, and to leave him and his demons alone! I obliged him, as I had my own demons I was trying to fight. I couldn't blame him. I had interrupted the peace in his home many times while having heated arguments with Danielle.

I reluctantly moved back to Las Vegas and tried to pick up the pieces of my life and start over again. Shadora was now eighteen, and we decided to be in a relationship. She was everything I had ever wanted in a woman, down to the size of her shoes. She was perfect. In the midst of us dating, the phone calls began to come in from Danielle again; and for the first time, it did not matter; and I was glad that I was finally over her. Shadora was definitely all that she said she was; she was trying to live a life according to biblical standards. We would spend hours on the phone every day, and every night at ten o' clock she would tell me good night because she had to pray. This really impressed me, and I thought if she was this devoted to God, I could only imagine how she would be toward me. Her parents seemed to approve of us dating, and after a year of dating, I made them aware of my intentions, and I asked her to marry me. She was so different from anyone I had ever been with. This girl would not even kiss me because she didn't want to deal with the possibility of what could happen. I wished that I had the willpower to do what she was doing. It is only hard to do the right thing when the desire to do the wrong thing is more desperately wanted than the urge to do right that is inside of you. I realize now that abstinence does not mean deliverance. There has to be a renewing of the mind in order to achieve some semblance of overcoming that which has a hold on you or to stop a behavior that you no longer wish to have. This can only be achieved through Jesus. I certainly haven't found another way. Shadora and I soon became inseparable. We planned our wedding, and the date was set for the month of September. We were waiting to have sex until we got married, and I was tested in a big way the weekend her parents left town and told me I could spend the night.

There is always a way to escape when you are tested. I was rubbing her back, and she said to me, "If you are going to keep rubbing me like that, you are going to have to marry me!" In other words, "Hands off, I'm not yours just yet." I called her on that demand, and we married. I now see I made the best decision I could have made as far as I was concerned. I would later have proof to substantiate my decision.

Chapter 3

MANY ARE CALLED BUT FEW ARE CHOSEN

In this book I share portions of my life candidly. Very private and intimate details of my life, as well as personal triumphs and tragedies. Through my own personal experiences, I can tell and hopefully convince you that no matter what you go through in this life, don't ever give up on God. You may let yourself down time and time again, but as long as you hold on, you can persist until you succeed. Somebody needs the differences that you have had in your life to make a difference in theirs. It's amazing how little your life has to do about you. We can rely on the experiences of others to find solace in the storms in our own lives, I believe.

After my grandmother died, my mom and all five of us kids moved back to Las Vegas. We were faced with some tough times. Momma had faith in Jesus, a positive outlook in life, a very vivid imagination, and an even stronger will—traits and qualities she passed on to us kids. We really had nowhere to go. We lived in an abandoned crack house that had no electricity and no running water. We had a roof over our heads, and that was a lot more than some people had. We considered ourselves blessed. My mother did the best she could, but there were times that all she had to nourish herself with was tea. With what food she could get together, we would have a hot meal.

The Bible lets us know that everyone is gifted in some way. Your gift is usually the talent or skill you possess, which may be similar to the skill or talent of someone else; but your particular gift, when executed, is uniquely different, not because of the response that you receive when you share it, but unique enough that one knows when it is yours. A unique attribute can be as simple as a name. The best things in life are free. You did not have to pay your parents for the name that they gave you at birth. It is free. On the same note, imagine the price you pay when your name is tarnished. And the amount of time and work it takes to have your name mean something again.

All comedians tell jokes; all chefs prepare food. When you are really ready to laugh, you don't want just any comedian; when you are really hungry, you don't want just any meal. You look for the product that is able to satisfy that which you desire. We all are consumers. We take in. It is in our makeup as humans. It is more blessed to give than to receive because it forces us to deviate from the norm. We all have a product, and people will receive it; and if you execute the giving of your product carefully and diligently, your product will sustain you. The Bible lets us know that our gift will allow us an audience before great men (Proverbs 18:16). Our gifts can and will often sustain us. You cannot just sit and wait on God to bless you. The product or gift that he has given you is designed to bless you. The product that is inside of you is as unique as you are. You may look like someone, act like someone, or even smell like someone; but you are not them and your product is yours.

When you have realized the gift you have, it is now time to begin to cultivate it. You begin to practice your product but, most importantly, know your product. That way, when it is time to display and give your product to others, success is nearly inevitable.

Many are called but few are chosen (Matthew 21:14). You may sing and be gifted in that area, and in this world, we have many singers, but your words are different, and so is the melody in your voice. Your voice can be imitated, but it cannot be duplicated. So what I am saying is this: you may have a similar talent as someone else, but the uniqueness of you makes it different. While we are cultivating our gift, we must find that thing that allows our product to be different while at the same time being synonymous with the original creation. Music is simply singing words, but the difference is what makes it worth listening to. That product or talent was given to many, but only a few pioneered the different genres that we love, such as country music and R & B. The music is very similar in some of the storylines in each song. They are both ways to sing, but the uniqueness of them makes it completely different. That is how we are as people. We are so much like each other but unique enough to be different and it is because of our product. So many people struggle needlessly because they have not recognized or failed to cultivate their gift. Be it situational, procrastination, or in-the-moment decision making.

Let's talk about Mary, the mother of Jesus. A virgin not yet knowing the pleasure of sexual intercourse is now chosen to carry the seed of God, being impregnated by the Spirit of God. Many women have wombs that are suitable for carrying a child, but the womb of Mary was chosen to be the nurturing edifice that Christ the King would inhabit for human formation. Some of us can take the tasks that we have been chosen to perform lightly, because it is common and is seen and done on a daily basis. People have children every day. However, this particular child would be the savior of the world, and his birth had to be.

Even though she was chosen by God, Mary had to choose to allow his plan to come forth. We all have a choice in life to carry out our purpose, the reason why we were created, our true reason for living. Just about any woman who has the ability to reproduce can become pregnant. However, forming in the wombs of some women is greatness. We all are important; no one is just here to populate the world. It seems we equate greatness with social status. The ability to reach many may make you popular, but it is your character that makes you great. A person can reach multitudes with a message; however, if that message is of hate or immorality, they have attained only popularity. The ability to share what is on the inside of you, though small in thought, can literally change the course of one's life. A simple hello to a person who is often overlooked and considered by most in society as not even being worthy of being spoken to can be a spark that lights a fire inside their heart and give them what they need to go on and become a spark in someone else's life. Suppose Mary, sitting one day pondering on the life that she must lead, facing the ridicule of everyone around her and hostile popularity, had decided this would be too much. Where would the billions of people who live and have lived in the world be without Jesus? It does not make sense; neither is it physically possible for a virgin to be pregnant. This part, as with many things in life, was out of her control.

God rewards obedience not just the results. We cannot be so concerned with the reaction of people when we are carrying out that which God has created us to do. It is not up to us to force anyone to do anything. Mary, though she loved her child Jesus, was not responsible for people's reaction to him. It was, however, her responsibility to raise and rear him. Nurturing is the biggest factor to be considered. The way you handle that in which you are chosen to govern. We will always have critics. One plants, one waters, but only God gives the increase. No one knows or, for that matter, can comprehend the ending of an intricate weaving of a plan woven by the master; so it is important to do what we are to do and not worry about the end result. It is up to God and the individual(s) it was created for to receive it after we have done our best in executing our gift.

Being concerned and worrying are two different things: worry will cause you to make rash decisions because you feel in yourself that you can correct a problem or give an end to a situation. That is not what we are here for. Concern, on the other hand, sparks curiosity, empathy, and more thought.

Consider, for example, if you were a farmer and you grow tomatoes that are sold to a sauce company. The sauce company sells their products to restaurants across the country; and in one of those restaurants, a waiter serves sauce made by your tomatoes to a customer; and because the customer doesn't like the tomato sauce, they want to send their entree back, that does not make you, the tomato farmer liable. No. Your job was to simply grow the tomatoes. What people do with them is not for you to worry about. Concern, yes, because you are critical of your tomatoes, but you cannot worry about the reactions of the one person who didn't like the sauce. You didn't make the sauce; you did your part and grew the tomatoes, and even though the one person didn't like the sauce that was made from your tomatoes, many others may have loved it. Suppose there was a family that sat around their dinner table; and because the meal was so delicious, they began to talk and laugh; and because of that, it brought them that much closer; and all that happened because a farmer grew his tomatoes. The point I am making is, it is more important that the farmer grew his tomatoes. His harvest may or may not have been what he wanted it to be; he could have faced many obstacles trying to till the field, had equipment failures, and so on (I equate this with the trials and tribulations we have in life), but it is what he is supposed to do, and the end results affect so many.

Don't get so caught up with praise and recognition from others. The things that are considered taboo or immoral are done in secret because it is in us to be seen as upstanding, moral, upright individuals. So to avoid the condemnation of our fellow humans, we would rather displease God. Understand that no one is ever going to be a better you than you are. If you don't do what you are supposed to do in your life, we all in some way miss out. Everyone is neglected by missing out on your contribution to an individual's life or society. You are worth more than just an employee in a company or just a mother or a father. Find the real you and express it as if your life depends on it. Someone's life very may well. It is important that you are an important part of your own life, community, and world. The impact of you doing so changes one person's world. Remember that you may never know the person you touch. Just be all of the you that you can.

Chapter 4

SHADORA

"Leave me, please, just leave me," I told my wife, Shadora. I figured that because she was young and beautiful, and she had already been through so much in her life, and the promises I made her while we were courting, concerning a future with me, seemed as though they may never be fulfilled. I felt like her being with me would somehow stifle her having the happy life that she deserved. Our worlds were completely turned upside down. I was experiencing situations and circumstances that left me feeling totally emasculated and overwhelmed. I was not able to do things in the conventional way that I thought a father and husband should operate.

My stepfather was the example that I had of a man, and I saw from him that you always sacrifice so your wife and kids don't go without, and do all you can to give them what they not only need but want. Not every man whose wife is good to him thinks they have a good woman who simply loves them no matter what. I am no exception to the rule. My wife was a young woman; however, she was raised with a lot of old-fashioned values, especially when it comes to her husband. Standing by your man no matter what and loving him unconditionally are two things that I have never had to worry about. People often told me how blessed I was that she was staying with me, because she was young and very pretty, and a lot of women would not stay in a relationship with a man after something as traumatic as what we were going through. When you love a person from a place where separation is not even an option, thoughts like that don't really enter into the mind of the one loving you. The thought of us breaking up never entered her mind; she never once thought of leaving me because I was now paralyzed. My wife says that she feels as though it is an honor to take care of me.

There was a nurse who I had established a pretty good rapport with. I really felt like she was a pretty good person, and I am not saying she is not; but one day she pulled my wife to the side, reaffirmed her age, youth, and beauty and bluntly told her to leave me. She went on to say that I was not going to ever get any better, and I would be of no use to her, and if anything, I would only hold her back in life, and she was too young to go through her life being with me. My wife was almost in tears. She was absolutely floored not just by the words the nurse said but also because she said them. We were out one day shopping and we ran into this nurse. Her eyes got as big as saucers and she could not say a word. My wife loves me, and not once have I heard her breathe hard in frustration or give me a cross look when I need her. Even when she had to be at work at four in the morning, I could wake her in the middle of the night for anything I needed and it would be done. She takes care of me. To say she takes care of me really seems to minimize things she does. When I could not feed myself, she fed me, and when I could not brush my own teeth, she did. She bathed me, dressed me, stayed up with me all night long while I was too sick to sleep, and she would get up in the morning and care for our son. This just did not happen once in a while; it was on an almost-daily basis. When I was in the hospital off and on sometimes for months, she would be there with me all day long and then go home and cook me dinner and bring it to me because I don't like hospital food.

I can honestly say she has never once complained. She was only eighteen when this happened to us, and after dealing with a similar situation with her mother and to still go on the way she does is awe inspiring. Juggling a small child, a home, a job, and a disabled husband who at times is demanding because of his condition—I applaud you, Shadora. You're amazing, baby, and I love you.

This has not been an easy journey; I just cannot seem to overcome myself. I'm married now, and so my successes and failures are no longer just my own but also my wife's and my child's. You see, I had major plans before I married my wife. I had major plans for us, and I had to, not only for myself but also for my eighteen-year-old wife. I had to make her father some serious promises before he would give his blessing to allow us to marry. It's a small world. I knew her father prior to meeting Shadora through a good friend who was his nephew. Her father thought I was a really good guy until the night I had a performance at the church she attended. I saw her and was immediately smitten. She was absolutely gorgeous. I always made it a habit to never mix my love life and ministry no matter how beautiful I thought the girl was. I never wanted the reputation of a whorish preacher. But this time it was different and I had to meet her. I thought she was a lot older than what she was, and it was not until later I found out her real age. Her father was not having it. Learning from my previous situation and not wanting to risk going to jail, I backed off as well.

When she became of age, we began to date. We were trying so hard to do things by the book; I mean it took us months of dating before she would even give me a kiss. At night after our elaborate dates, she would just give me a booty hug (you know the way you hug someone of the opposite sex when you're trying not to make any body contact and you stick your booty out—I call that a booty hug). And she would send me on my way. I went all out for our dates. I was working two jobs and had no kids; I had the money to spend. There was something special about her, and I had to capture her interest. Most of my working life, even when I was younger, I would buy my mother a dress and shoes nearly every payday so I would be prepared when I found that special lady and married. So one night I finally wore her down, and she kissed me—and oh what a kiss it was. She later told me that the reason she did not want to do anything even semi sexual, not even listening to sensual love songs, was because she was trying to live saved and please God; and as a single woman, she did not want her mind to wander.

Premarital sex was out of the question. After we began to date, her father and stepmother approved of me because I was so respectful to their child, and my intentions were admirable, and I respected them and their rules concerning her even though legally she was an adult. I did what was right. She wanted to as well. Eventually we married.

Being disabled has not been easy for me, and I just knew that this situation had to be physically, mentally, and emotionally difficult for her. I really felt like she was being shorted, robbed even, of a good life because she was also the product of a broken home; and if that was not enough, she had to suffer abuse at the hands of her mother when she was a child. Shadora was born premature. She was only about two pounds, and she used to wear the clothes of baby dolls. When she was seven years old, her parents divorced, and the abuse only got worse. Members of Shadora's family often treated and dealt with her as a second-class citizen, and she loved them dearly in spite of it. She had other siblings that her family placed on a pedestal, especially her older sister, who is the spitting image of her mother. Her mother, lovesick, began to have a series of strokes, which left her partially paralyzed. Shadora, along with her siblings, now had to care for their mother. It would be so tedious that at times she felt guilty for feeling relief when her mother would be too sick to stay home and had to go into the hospital. There was even an episode where their home caught fire, and in the haste of self-preservation, everyone left their crippled mother in the house, and Shadora ran back in to save her. This eighty-pound thirteen-year-old girl carried her two-hundred-plus-pound mother to her wheelchair and out of the burning house.

Eventually the diabetes, high blood pressure, and strokes began to take over; and Shadora's mother eventually became a total vegetable, unable to walk or talk. This is the condition her mother was in when I met her. We would visit her quite often, and with the exception of one aunt, she really had no visitors other than Shadora. When we would visit her, she occasionally tried to communicate; but most of the time she would turn her head, as if even in her current state of health we were bothering her or she was agitated by Shadora's presence. I never thought much of it because of the state her mother was in, until one day her sister, whom everyone loved so much, came with us on one of our many visits. When we walked in the room, her mother did something that totally amazed me. When she finally recognized that her other daughter, was there, she lit up like a Christmas tree, trying to communicate with her. It was baffling, but I figured it was because she had not seen her in so long. I had never seen her mother act in such a way. I chalked it up to nothing until it happened once more, and then I realized that her mother's dislike for her was so strong that it continued on even through all this, and although my wife knew it, she never stopped coming to see her mother.

I remember walking ahead of her one day. I said I needed a few moments alone with her mother. I went into the room where her mother lay almost lifeless, and I told her, "Shadora is about the only person who cares enough to come and see about you because she loves you and she cares, and it is hurtful even in this state that you would treat her with indifference. It's not right, and please stop." Things kind of changed for a short while, and she seemed to be okay. We asked her if she approved of us dating, and she surprisingly said yes, but soon she returned to her old cantankerous ways. Even in her present state, she knew what was going on around her, even though she could not speak

After a while, I knew Shadora was it and that she was the one I wanted to marry. I wanted to love her deeply, so deep and true that it would erase all of the hurt from her past, love her in a place that seemingly no one had loved her before. A place that could make her forget about all that had happened or at least show her she was worthy of being treated with love. Her mother, being ill all that time, was preparation for what she would be faced with later on in life with her own husband. Oftentimes we wonder why things happen to those we love so dearly; we have to understand that there is a plan for our existence and not try to figure the plan out—just know that no one is here just to exist. Each of our lives is partly for the betterment of someone else. As I look back on that method of thinking, I now know I really gave myself too much credit. Thinking you can erase emotional scars is foolish. What needs to be concentrated on is not creating any new ones. So as time went on, we grew closer, spending all of our time together. We were friends, we prayed together, we laughed together—everything. So one night I announced my intentions to Shadora's father and stepmother. Her stepmother was okay with it, but her father wanted me to wait, not for his daughter's sake, surprisingly enough, but for mine. He was emphatic that she was not ready, she did not know what she was getting into, and she was not ready to care for a home. He knew his daughter far better than I, but we did not heed the warnings, as bizarre as they seemed, and we continued to plan our wedding. I thought that what she did not know I would have to teach her, and it was worth it because we really wanted to be married. We were not having sex, and we were young and in love, and we were human, and, well, hormones are something else.

Her parents trusted me to do what was right, so one weekend they went out of town, and they invited me to stay at their home while they were gone. I accepted. So there we were lying in bed to go to sleep. I was holding her in my arms and we were talking. I began to rub her back, and she did not tell me to stop; she only told me if I continued to rub her back that I would need to marry her. That's one of the times I was glad I lived in a twenty-four-hour town. I did not know if she was bluffing or not, but I called her on it, and we went downtown and we did just that. I never proposed to her; it was just spoken between us that we would be married. We decided to keep it just to ourselves and still go on with the ceremony we had been planning, and none would be the wiser. People had suspicions because she began to spend the night at my house and my friends and family just could not believe what I was doing, especially after knowing how I lived. What was I doing having this girl spend the night? We were doing a good job. I was making plans to find us a house and a nice car because she did not drive, and I was finally going to have my Chrysler 300. I went to tell Shadora what we were getting, and that is when she told me she was pregnant. Wow, I did it again. The wedding was too far away to keep this a secret any longer, so we told everyone what we had done.

Chapter 5

I Didn't Find My Life until I Almost Lost It

My wife and I began our lives together in a condo that I shared with my brother, and eventually my sister and her three kids moved in, and my wife said she needed her own space. Prior to her moving out, I asked my in-laws to allow my wife to remain at home for a few months while I got a place for us. I really could have handled this situation better. To me they really seemed glad that I was taking her off their hands. My mother-in-law, who is very well versed in matters of the heart, said to me, "That's your wife. Take her with you." I was so very offended, and that is what helped me draw that conclusion. My mother-in-law could not have been more right. Not that it would have made any difference, but I am glad I didn't persist. So finally we got an apartment in one of the more prominent areas of town that we thought would be safer than where we lived and a great place to raise a family. I was working two jobs just like I had been taught, and Shadora's going to school. I promised her father that she would continue on to college just like we had planned.

We had mutual friends, James and Gladys, who we often hung out with. They were married before we were. They lived with friends, and the relationship between them and the friends soured, and they asked to live with us for a while, which was fine because we viewed them as sister and brother. They tried to find an apartment in the same complex as us, but there were no vacancies, so they moved directly across the street. You could look out of our front door and see their place and vice versa.

On November 20, 2004, my wife had to go to a debutante reunion ball, and I didn't want to go because I didn't have a tuxedo, and I would feel out of place. That same night, James's wife was having a slumber party, and all of her girlfriends would be over, and James didn't want to be there for that, so we agreed he would stay the night at my house. James and I went out that night to a casino, which had a club in it, and we walked down to see what it was all about. I had never been one for nightclubs, but we met some girls there, and we danced a few songs, and he had a drink and then we left. We stopped at a fast-food joint. I got a phone call from my best friend, Teisha, and we talked for a few minutes, and then we went to my home. We watched TV in the living room, and eventually the hour began to get late. I gave James a blanket so he could sleep on the couch. I went to bed in my room, closing the door behind me.

About three o'clock that morning, we got a phone call from James's wife, asking us if we had seen him. My wife woke me up to ask me if I had seen James, and I said, "Yeah, he's on the couch sleeping," because that's where I had left him. My wife got up and proceeded into the living room to give James the phone and, to our surprise, no James. He hadn't woken us to say he was leaving or at least to lock the door—nothing. So my wife told James's wife that he wasn't out there, and we had no idea where he was. The last time I saw him was that night in the living room, going to sleep. I passed it off as nothing major, and that was it until my wife called James's wife some time later and asked if she had seen him yet. I guess Gladys was up waiting for him and she said, "I'm looking out my front door, and I see James on your stairs with three other people, but I don't know who they are." Soon they were knocking at my front door.

I was still in bed asleep when my wife asked James who those people were with him. He said, "Its fine. Don't worry about them, just open the door." So she did, and when James and the other two guys and a girl came in, my wife said the biggest guy snatched her phone out of her hand. She snatched it back and ran to our bedroom, where James was trying to wake me by shaking me and shouting, "Wake up! Help me! These guys are trying to rob me!" While still drowsy, I jumped to my feet to defend my pregnant wife and who I thought was my friend. There were three of them, and I saw that one had a gun so I said to them, "This is a holy house, and in Jesus's name, I want you all to leave." Until recently I always thought that my announcement didn't work because I got shot. I never thought about the fact that after they shot me, they ran from my home. Those people had murder on their minds that night, and this situation could have been a lot worse than how it ended. They knew they had shot me because when I was hit by the bullet I yelled, "I'm hit!" Once they knew that, they could have come on in and finished the job.

After I said, "This is a holy house and in Jesus's name I want you to leave," I closed my bedroom door, and James was hiding behind my wife. I leaned against the door so they couldn't get in, and that is when two shots rang out, and one hit me in the arm. Shortly thereafter, I fell to the floor involuntarily; and when I tried to get back up, I couldn't. I said, "I can't feel my legs!" James said, "You're just in shock."

It was pandemonium in the house after that. Soon the police showed up, and an officer had to kick my bedroom door in because when they shot me I fell where I was standing. When the officer came in the room, he had his gun drawn, and though I was lying on the floor bleeding, I quickly yelled, "I'm the victim!" The cop tried to help me up, and when he couldn't, he just held my head until the paramedics showed up. The next thing I remember was in the trauma unit at the hospital, and I was having a tube placed in my chest to drain the fluid from my lung. The bullet that entered my arm bruised my lung and severed my spine. I was only shot once. I was drugged for weeks, and the days just kind of ran together.

I will never forget the day the doctor came in my room. I was semiconscious; he ran a pencil over my upper chest and asked me if I felt the pencil, and I replied, "Yes." He then slid the pencil on my stomach and asked me the same question, and I said, "No." Lastly, he slid the pencil over my foot and asked if I felt that, and again I said, "No." He then replied, "You won't be walking anymore," and walked out of the room. He didn't even look at me when he said it. I have never felt so all alone in the world in my entire life; he said it with absolutely no compassion. I did not know that I was getting ready to endure so much more of this type of attitude from people, especially in the health-care field. Being fat, you face discrimination. Being black, you face so much discrimination. Now place being crippled on top of that. I remember being in one hospital where they asked the janitor to come help turn me.

When this first happened, I originally had private health insurance through my job, and once that lapsed because I was not working, I then had to get state-paid insurance, which only added fuel to the fire. I have been treated horribly by medical professionals, especially when they feel like they are doing you a favor. I mean, when you are already in a position of helplessness and you are made to feel like your presence is an imposition, it is hard to concentrate on getting better. Anytime you work on a job, it can get tedious, but people need to realize that patients are oftentimes frightened. Being in hospitals can be very intimidating, and hospitals are already very intimidating and frightful places, especially to people who aren't often or have never been hospitalized. No two people are the same, and neither should they be treated that way. Compassion should be emphasized, not sporadically given because of a person's status. I was in and out of hospitals and rehabilitation facilities for about a year. I was more than ready to go home, but the only problem was I had no home to go to. For the second time in my life, I was homeless. The apartment I had been shot in was out of the question. My parents lived in a senior community, and my in-laws couldn't figure out how much rent they wanted my wife to pay when she was pregnant and needed a place, and they wouldn't give her a place to stay, so I knew us all living there was completely out of the question. We had no place to go until my best friend, Teisha, stepped up to the plate. That is when she told me that we were all coming to live with her.

Teisha is married and has three children, my goddaughters; they had a three-bedroom home. Teisha and her husband, Darien, moved all of their girls into one room; and my wife and my child and I all shared one room. I had a hospital bed, and my wife slept on a mattress on the floor with my child; we did this for one year exactly. Two families in one house, and we never argued or disagreed on a serious level. Even with the nurses, doctors, and therapist coming in and out of her home, Teisha never complained. People say friends should never live together, and after this situation, I must say I disagree; we did and are still friends to this day, closer than ever. Darien and I grew even closer, and a brotherhood is now there.

Throughout this entire ordeal, I have never had to want for anything, and I attribute that to always being a giver. I always gave tithe and offering in church, but my giving went further than that. I gave to individuals every chance I got. My company held a fund-raiser for me and so did some local churches. The fund-raiser was themed Trust the Process. When I was in the hospital, different patients would hear about my story, and they began to write me checks. Within six months, I had an entire year's salary just from gifts and donations.

When I joined the church I now attend, the congregation was like family, so when we would have different evangelists come in, instead of the church having the expense of hotel accommodations, I would offer up my apartment, which was nicer than some of these hotel rooms even on the strip.

When the time came and I was strong enough, my wife and I started looking for our own place, but we just couldn't find a place that suited our needs. I needed a room just to house all the equipment and supplies that I had to have just for basic daily living. I had just filed for bankruptcy, and my wife had only been on her job for about three days. My only income was $888 a month in social security, and we had the nerve to go and apply for a mortgage. Of course we were turned down; however, one night I began to pray, and I reminded God that I had always given my apartment when the evangelists came into town to preach. I gave up my apartment and went and slept on the floor at my pastor's house so the church wouldn't have the expense. "God, now my family and I need a place to live and we need it now." You see, it wasn't as if I did all those things, looking for something in return; I did them because my heart said so. You have to remind God of the promises he has made to his children, not because he has forgotten but rather to increase your faith.

At this point, faith was all we had. We had gone through all of our money just living. We applied for one last loan. We met with a realtor, who wanted us to talk to a loan officer she used, but we could never get a hold of him, so we went through a different loan officer. The loan officer came to the house we were living in and gathered all of our information. When she was finished, she examined all the figures that were in front of her and she said, "There is just no way can you all be approved for a loan." However, I knew what I had prayed and was holding on. She gave our file to her supervisor, and after she examined it, she had to agree that there was nothing she could do to help us. That is when our prayer for a home was answered. The Lord moved upon her heart, and after she said all of that, she followed it up with, "But I have a son, and he also was just married. This Severs family is living with a family, and these people have a child, and they can't live in that room forever. I would want someone to give my child a chance. I am going to give them a chance. I don't know why I feel like there is something different about them."

That bank then gave us a loan for $185,000! We had the money, and now we couldn't find a house anywhere. We were outbid for every home we bid on; then one night I grabbed the phone book, and before I began to thumb through the real estate section, I prayed again. I called a real estate company and somehow talked to the owner, and after a short while, we found a home that had already been modified with wheelchair accessibilities. We moved in with no money down, the homeowners paid our closing cost, and we ended up getting a check for over a thousand dollars at closing. What a *mighty* God we serve! My wife went back to work when our son was about ten months old, and

I kept our son during the day by myself. I only had use of one hand, and I changed diapers and made bottles. I even potty trained him in about a month. When you accept the things in life that you must do and figure out a way, anything is possible.

The most valuable lesson I have learned is an old but true cliché. Prayer changes things!

Chapter 6

LOOK FOR THE BIGGER PICTURE

We finally had our own place, and things were looking up for us. I began to reassess my life and tried to go back to work. I could be in perfect health until the day that I would get up and get ready to go for a job interview. Something medically would always happen to land me back in the hospital. I didn't look at it as something happening to hinder me in a negative way, rather than a diversion to keep me on the path to receive the things that I needed from God, the path that he had for me. The decision I was making to go back to work would not allow me to be in the position to reach the people that I would like to. That I have to. There are dreams I have not attained, but I am hoping that this book will be a start. I did a comedy comeback show, and I thought it went well, but I received no response from it. So I am this time going by the direction of the Lord. I am following by much prayer and working in the gifts that I have within me. The title of this book came simply from a thought the Lord placed on my heart. I really believe in Jesus, and through him there is redemption from sin. The purpose for his mother, Mary's life was to bring forth Jesus. She experienced life's pleasures and displeasures just like we all do. She was shown no special privileges by God according to the story; she gave birth to Jesus in a stable with no relief from labor pains and no special attention by the Catholic Church until after her death.

We have to allow our lives to be vehicles for the betterment of ourselves and others. Though we have talents that we enjoy, if we share them with others we all can receive the benefits of that and find similar happiness. We must live our lives to attain personal happiness, but a lot of that comes through the satisfaction we receive from helping someone else. By sharing our gift, whether it is with an individual or the world, one person can change the world just like one person can change someone's world. Just be you. You are needed. Think of the people who have had an impact on your life, whether great or small. Now imagine if they had allowed selfishness or fear to prevent them from touching your life as they did. You may never know the impact you have on some people, but it is there and it's real.

Christ gave his life so that we all can have freedom—freedom of the mind. Our minds are so powerful, and we have the ability to decipher right from wrong, pleasure from pain. We can do something, but if our mind is not in agreement with it, our body will not even enjoy it. My own life seems like it has been set up for destruction since I entered this earth. Just like God has a plan for our lives, so does the enemy. There are two powers that beat beneath your breast—one you love and one you hate, but the one you follow will dominate. I could have beat myself over the head about the decisions I have made or the horrible things that have happened to me, but my mind won't allow it. I think my life is one of the worst ones you ever want to hear about. Another person may think their life is. There comes a time when you must look past yourself and think of the lives that your experiences will touch. I don't think that I deserve children because I have murdered three children through abortion. However, God didn't hold that against me, and I was blessed with a beautiful son. Not because I deserve it but because I do believe he forgave me. My son's life is going to help others, and it already has. If nothing else, his life has shown me about the forgiving power of Jesus.

My body has gone through so many things since this happened to me. I have had wounds all over my body, some full of life-threatening infection and so deep you could look at them and see the bone. When I was shot, I was standing in my bedroom behind the door, and I was pressed against the door, leaning on my arm, so that if the intruders pushed into our bedroom, my weight would make it difficult for them when they tried to enter. I was shot in the arm and one of the bullets flew by my wife's head and entered one of the posts of our bed. I still have and sleep in that bed. (People ask if the memory of looking at the bullet hole bothers me, but I let them know that bed cost me almost two thousand dollars. I'll be all right!)

I fell and broke my left leg and ankle from the fall. When the police came, they could not get into the room because I was lying on the floor, and they had to kick the door in; consequently, my leg and ankle were broken. My leg healed, but my ankle didn't, and the doctors told me there was no need to fix it because I was not walking and didn't really need to use the ankle. If I had it fixed, I ran the risk of losing it because infection could attack my leg and bone. Now over time, my ankle bone has disintegrated, and I ended up getting infections in that ankle bone and left leg, and I had no ankle in my leg. Now the same doctors who said my leg would be fine like that say there is nothing to do but amputate it. I had, at one point, thirty-one different open wounds all over my body, mainly on my legs.

It has taken time, but I have forgiven the people who have done this to me. One day while in prayer, I asked God, "Why me?" And he said, "Why not?" We as individuals are no greater than anyone else. *Some face challenges of the body, some face challenges of the mind, and others face both—but we all must go through difficult times.*

He let me know that sometimes you have to take one for the team. I can attribute that to seemingly senseless things that happen, but they somehow better mankind. I thought it was so unfair. That's when he told me, "How can anything be unfair when you serve a just God?"

All my life I have been taught to pray to find God's will. When I met my wife, I was crazy about her. I prayed and asked the Lord, "Is this for me?" For weeks I prayed and received no answer. Then one morning in the shower, I heard the voice of the Lord say to me, "If you were walking down the street and found a million dollars, would you have asked me, 'Is this for me?' before you spent it? He then responded, No, you wouldn't." Sometimes the Lord doesn't answer with a simple yes or no; sometimes his answer is giving you what you need. I needed a wife who could mentally handle the ups and downs of caring for someone. A portion of her mother's life was set aside to prepare her for me. His plans of life are so intricate.

I would not wish what I have gone through on the people who have done this to me. One day in anger, I asked God, "Why don't you just kill James?" He said, "Brandon, my child, James repented to me, and I am his God also, and the same forgiveness that you would have wanted to be shown if the roles were reversed I showed to James. No one is greater than anyone else, and though our actions may be noble or dishonorable, we are all able to be forgiven." Now that doesn't mean that James won't receive judgment for his actions, but that is why vengeance is reserved by God for God. It is when we believe that we can execute vengeance based on our emotions that we can place ourselves in sticky situations; the best vengeance that we have for anyone is forgiveness. Our vengeance might bring us pleasure for a while or allow us to feel that justice was served, but the vengeance of God can cause you to pray for your enemy. Be not deceived. God is not mocked. Whatever a man soweth, that shall he also reap.

Do you know that you are the best person God ever created? Seriously, if you ask yourself or someone else that question, they may answer no, but they may have a smile on their face. That's because the heart knows the truth. We can change one's emotional status, we have that power, but only God can give joy; that's when you smile for no reason, laugh because you can, or have peace of mind in times of a storm. Now that's joy and that comes from God.

The ability to forgive and see that even though someone has brought you harm or turned your life upside down, you can forgive, is not a human attribute. That comes from the one and only up above. Since my life has been like this, it has slowed me down greatly, so my life didn't end in a shipwreck but, rather, take a course of nonselfishness for others.

I don't live my life to please others, but I know the decisions I make affect not only me, which allows me to decipher much more diligently my decision-making process. If you kill a man, you are just not stopping his life. You have not only killed him but now have inflicted possible life-altering pain and emotional assault to a possible father, mother, wife, aunts, uncles, cousins, children, friends, coworkers, and community. No decision you make ever affects the life of only one person. Even if a man wants to do something special for his wife and buy her a gift, everyone who has any part in that gift is affected. The man might go to a jewelry store, and in that store there are employees. By buying the ring, the man has brought revenue to that company, which allows the company to grow and allows the employee to have a check to pay for things for their family, all because of the decision he made. It affected so many lives, and he may have just thought he was buying a gift.

Chapter 7

LIVING WITH A DISABILITY

There are so many limits placed on people with disabilities by others and themselves. I have often wondered what things I could have done or accomplished had I not been told that I couldn't or wouldn't or would face extreme difficulties doing things that were everyday normal activities that I did before I became "disabled." It has often been said that illness is mental. Now that I have experienced illness and disability firsthand, I see that it is the rehabilitation process after illness or disability that is mental. You can be very positive and optimistic, but if something is malfunctioning biologically, the body must repair itself, and positive thinking can aid in this unless you are healed miraculously.

The mind was never designed for failure. It was made for servitude and protection for a lifetime. A portion of our mind was made to send messages to various parts of our bodies and expects complete obedience for that which it has commanded—nothing more, nothing less. It protects us by allowing us to feel pain when there is something wrong. If we need a part of our body to perform a task and it doesn't, we tend to compensate by turning to another part of our body for that. I believe the same happens in life; if there is something that must be accomplished by an individual and they don't do it, a replacement is often sent to do it.

Oftentimes we limit ourselves with obstacles that seem insurmountable. If it is for you to accomplish, it is in you to accomplish it. Believe that success is as much a part of you as the nose on your face. The mind is the most powerful tool we have. A gun is powerful, and the bullets inside can kill, but if the idea of creation of the gun never entered into the mind, its creation would be nonexistent, so I ask which is mightier.

You cannot give into limits. There is a difference between coming to grips with something and accepting it. I was shot, and the bullet severed my spine, and I am now in a paralyzed condition. I have not accepted it. I have come to terms with it. That means for some semblance of a quality life, I am going to have to do the things necessary to live as comfortably as I can while I am in this state. For instance, I have a wheelchair to move about in, and I have a van that has been modified to accommodate a wheelchair so that I can travel. However, I believe in the miracle-working power of Jesus Christ, and it is in that name that I have faith that he will one day work a miracle and heal me, and I will be healed and get up out of this wheelchair walking, as opposed to accepting this medical diagnosis, which will leave me totally paralyzed. Accommodate yourself with comfort ability while in a situation, do whatever it takes to achieve it, and while you're in a situation, accept all that is there for you to aid in your comfort ability until accomplishment is met.

If I didn't have this faith, I would be totally depressed, allowing frustration and sadness to keep me down. Not saying that I haven't dealt with bad days or discouragement, because I have trials and tribulations that are often as seasonal as weather changes, as you do while living with disability. It can be difficult and downright depressing trying to function in a normal capacity when you are disabled. Many people are overwhelmed to the point of a depression that often leads to suicide. Some, though, accept their diagnosis and continue on wonderfully. There is so much that you deal with when you have a disability, things I had no idea I would ever encounter, and I definitely did not know what people in wheelchairs dealt with. Normally when I saw a person in a wheelchair, I didn't give it much thought other than a fleeting, "How'd that happen?" When I was first shot, I went to a trauma center—no surgery. My injury was deemed a "complete." With spinal cord injuries, you have "completes," where the spinal cord is completely severed, and "incomplete," where the spine is only partially severed, and there is normally some sort of trace movement throughout the body, often coupled with extreme nerve pain, muscle spasm, etc. I wasn't in the hospital for a year because of the gunshot wound that I sustained but, rather, the complications I had from the doctors and nurses trying to get me acclimated to life in a chair.

I was fitted for a plastic brace that wrapped around my upper torso. This was supposed to act in place of my spine and give me the upper body stability that I no longer had because of the injury to my spinal cord. I was paralyzed from my nipples down. (I have always considered this as God having a sense of humor. I haven't met or heard of anyone paralyzed from that level! Though I hear it is common.) And for a while I could not move any parts of my body. I couldn't sit up or hold myself up—my body was basically like a limp pasta noodle. On one occasion, after the therapy that they would give me in the bed, they didn't take the brace off me afterward. With the only thing I could do being to lie down, the pressure from the brace became too great for my body, and my skin began to break down. Sores began to develop that eventually turned into huge gaping holes on my back, holes that were several inches in width and depth and nearly covered my entire back. Once, the wounds became life-threatening when they became infected. The smell coming from these wounds was horrific. The wounds were so great that the doctor had to put a vacuum system called a wound VAC on them. The wound VAC applied a constant sucking therapy to the area to aid with bringing the healthy skin tissue to the surface and keeping the fluids that were constantly draining from these wounds off them.

I used to dread the day when it was time to change these dressings. I would have to be turned on my side, and it would take hours because the wounds were so great in size, and it was extremely painful to lie on my side for that amount of time. I was supposed to be turned from side to side to relieve pressure from my body to avoid my skin breaking down in any more areas and keep any new wounds from forming, but with the subpar care I was receiving, they weren't doing this, and I developed wounds on my legs and feet. Some of the areas were so deep that the bone was exposed. I had constant urinary tract infections that became as normal as hangnails, even more so for me because I have an indwelling catheter and so urinary tract infections are inevitably going to happen even if you don't have an indwelling catheter and have incontinence issues. A lot of people with spinal cord injuries do something called straight cathing. That's when each time you have to urinate you must stick a catheter inside your penis or vagina until it reaches your bladder and the urine drains out.

When I originally came home from the hospital, my older brother and my wife cared for me. They took care of my meal preparation, toilet, bathing, grooming, transfers from bed to my wheelchair, etc. Later I was told about a personal care attendant (PCA). I had no idea that the state would pay for someone to care for me. I would later find out that this is a blessing and a curse. Some of these people are really great; they take pride in their jobs and have a genuine concern for the person or persons for whom they are caring. However, you have some that abuse drugs and are thieves and use this job as an opportunity for an easy high by stealing the medication prescribed for their patient. Or they are extremely lazy and show up to work at their convenience, knowing that the client is depending on them to eat or bathe or get dressed and make it to a doctor's appointment. I have experienced both. My wife's wedding ring mysteriously came up missing, and the only ones in the house where myself, my wife, my son, and my PCA.

People sometimes prey on vulnerable or helpless people; you end up feeling uncomfortable in your own home. When you have a disability, you must learn to adapt to life under some of the most strenuous conditions. At times it can be like reverting all the way back to infancy stages as a full-grown adult. I had to relearn to feed myself, wash my face, comb my hair, brush my teeth, and even write.

I did want some sort of repayment from the people who did this to me, but I wouldn't wish this on my worst enemy, not even the ones who caused it. In some sense, although I am not in a hospital, I still must deal with doctors, and I still have nurses who come and see me every day. I am grateful I have them because I would be in a worse state without them. So I deal with the frustration better when I consider the alternative—being confined to a hospital; having limited hours to see my wife and son, family, and friends; greater restrictions on my freedom; and all the others things that come along with hospitalization. So no matter how bad a situation seems, always consider the negative alternative and be grateful that you are there and consider the positive alternative and strive for it.

The old saying "Things could be worse" never brought me much solace because I was so angry about this situation. I didn't want to hear anything but "You're healed." Once you realize that this is the way things are, love life the same even with these challenges. I was really glad that things weren't worse than they were. I can laugh about it now. I had a friend who once told me the parable of "I complained I had no shoes until I saw a man who had no feet to use," and I angrily replied, "Why the hell would you complain about shoes if you have no feet!" So whatever you are faced with, learn to make it work for you; get everything that you have coming to you because of your new state of being, and love life the way it is. Things really could be worse, and thank goodness they're not.

One of the reasons I decided to write this book was to let people know that hanging on is worth it. When you experience a life-changing situation that is negative, everything that follows doesn't have to be. A positive attitude is a must. It is a requirement if you expect to have any sense of happiness in your life. The things that once brought you happiness may no longer be an option to you. So you must find happiness through different avenues. Remain realistic yet optimistic, and most importantly, hold fast to your faith.

I have had to live this way, and that is the reason I recommend this so strongly. I have had to live like this since I learned the obstacle now facing me. I remember when my son was about a year and a half old. My son means more to me than life itself and at times was the only reason I felt I had for living. One day he was in the living room playing by himself and really having a good time, and he wanted me to join him. He called out, "Daddy!" I answered, and he asked me to come play with him. I was in the bed and obviously could not get up and come. After Junior called for me several times and I didn't come, he walked over to the bed where I was lying, grabbed my arm, and began to pull, begging me to come with him. "Daddy, please come on!" And I couldn't. I cried for two days. I was absolutely crushed. I don't think I have ever felt pain like that before; my son simply wanted me to come and play with him, and I couldn't. My heart was so heavy because I knew this was not the last time this would happen, and I wanted to be able to play with my son. I haven't even been able to pick him up ever and hold him. After the two days of being hurt and crying, I began to play with my son in my bed and roll him balls if he was on the floor, and he was so happy, and I must say so was I.

That day I realized if I am not going to be able to do something the way I want to, I am going to figure out a way to do it differently, and I am going to do it. You owe it to yourself to figure out what works for you to achieve what you want and want to do. Don't forget, even though the disability is affecting your body, it is still *your* body. You are in charge although you are faced with adversity. Choose to live and do what it takes to enjoy this journey as much as you can while you can.

My life will one day no longer be like this. I believe that, and that is ultimately my driving force. That is what will keep me going until I take my first step, so for now I will continue to live. I may not know what the future holds, but I know who holds the future, and because of my faith in him, I can share with the world that hope is real. If you hang in there, a change will come. Even if the way you are disabled doesn't change, learn to live well with it. At times things will come along to shake your faith at its very core or foundation. But remember that old toy where the slogan said, "Weebles wobble but they don't fall down"? No matter how positive you remain, don't be so naive to think that life freezes and negative occurrences no longer exist, because they do and the harder you try and hang on, the harder it often seems, but anything worth having is worth fighting for.

Discouragement is just an emotion and is fleeting and doesn't have to last. So if you want to cry, cry. If you need to scream, scream—whatever it takes to *legally* give yourself release, do it. Then reaffirm to yourself what it is you're going for, and with all you've got, go after it because you're worth fighting for, and nothing beats a failure but a try.

Chapter 8

FORGIVENESS

Forgiveness is one of the hardest yet most important of all life's lessons. When a person has wronged you to the point that you must forgive them, the situation is not always one that is extremely major. However, if not acted on in a timely fashion, it can grow and fester to the point that it may have adverse effects on the relationship and, at times, the health of the individual who needs to forgive. One can hold a grudge toward another, and the person they haven't forgiven may not even know they have something against them. The Bible often speaks of forgiveness and its importance, so much so that if we don't forgive one another, God will not forgive us for our wrongdoings. When someone wrongs you and you do not forgive them, you give up control not only of that situation but of your emotions and, to an extent, a portion of your life. When someone has wronged you and you are harboring rescindment there is a part of you that has trouble visiting that place in your mind. What should be pleasant thoughts in your mind have now been replaced with ill feelings and possibly hatred.

When I was chosen to go through this situation, I experienced dealing with forgiveness in a new and awesome way. When a person wrongs you, whether it is intentional or inadvertent, and you don't forgive, they have taken a small portion of you; and the only way to get that piece of you back is through forgiveness. That person is continually on your mind; you are more than likely retelling the incident to anyone who will listen. It is constantly replaying in your head, and thoughts of retaliation may even be present. The what-ifs begin, and you think of things that you could have done differently. You are spending so much time and mental energy on this person and situation that it often consumes you. This consuming may be so extreme that you are now at the point where you are harboring ill feelings toward this individual. Now if you were to die while feeling like this, that person has controlled your life even unto death and now the afterlife. The Bible says that if we don't forgive others for the wrongs that they do to us, God will not forgive us for our wrongdoings. It can seem so unfair at times. Don't be deceived. Vengeance is not always handed out in the way that we feel it should according to our thoughts. It is reserved for God. However, when we intervene and take vengeance into our own hands, we tie God's hands and leave ourselves open for vengeance for wronging that person. Remember, no one is greater than another to God; we just have different positions and titles in life, no matter how heinous we feel a person are in the sight of God. If you steal five cents or five million dollars in the sight of God, the amount matters not compared to the act of stealing itself. God loves all sinners and hates all sin. Do not concern yourself with that person being repaid for what they did wrong as opposed to forgiving them and moving on with your life. All of it or the part of it that has already been stolen while you were wronged—keep what is left and make the most of it for you.

James may have consequently stolen my ability to walk, but he won't control my emotions, especially when he doesn't even know he is. I once heard a preacher say, "If we have to reap all that which we have sown, I am going to pray for crop failure!" What a true statement. There are so many things that I have done that are between me and God. That's all, and I wish to leave it there.

I harbored a lot of hurt and ill will toward my father. He was dead and gone, and I couldn't get an explanation as to why. He was gone, and there I was holding all this toward him, and the only real thing I could do was forgive him. Was he sorry? I may never know, but it is over now, and that is how I must see it—as over. Nothing can ever be done about it. Why get an ulcer or be stressed and unhappy about how he did me while living when his death symbolized it being over? No longer can he hurt me. As a person I won't give a feeling or a person that much power. If I do that, he has had a part of my emotions through life and now death, and no one deserves that much control.

It took much prayer and an "I don't think so" attitude to get over what has had to happen in my life. Although I can no longer walk, I am so much better in so many ways. I feel like I am closer to God. I have spent hours in prayer and reading my Bible, really having a chance to spend quality time with the Lord, which is important to me and offers me great solace and peace. God is so awesome; if you talk to him, he'll answer back. You just have to be quiet enough to listen. I believe this situation has saved my marriage. I can be a very flighty person because I hate conflict. I don't like to argue, and rather than do so, I will just leave a person, a situation, whatever, I will go. Once when my wife and I were first married, we were arguing, and whatever it was about had to be pretty unimportant because I don't even remember what the argument was about. She was in full swing, and I had made up in my mind what I was going to say, and after I said it, I decided that I was going to storm out of the front door and be gone for a while so she could see how mad she had made me. So finally it was my turn, and boy was I getting ready to let her have it, so I said what I had to and turned my wheelchair around and headed for the front door. But as much as I struggled, I couldn't get it open, so I turned to her and said, "Can you open the door please!" Needless to say I realized again how much I would need my wife, and we need to forgive and not act out with so much of the theatrics.

As far as my son goes, I think I have been a father like no other. I had never wanted kids; after all the abortions, I felt I wasn't worthy. For my wife to watch me get shot and be at the point of death and still carry the baby full term was a blessing in itself. I call him my miracle baby. The bond that my son and I have is simply amazing. I love this little boy so much it is ridiculous. All these things may not have even been so if I didn't have to stay there and take it. When I felt like running, I had no other choice but to literally sit there and take it, and it has made me a better man, Christian, husband, and father. God bless James. Don't get me wrong, I give no accolades to him for what he caused me, but because I was able to forgive him and remove those ill feelings from my heart, I had room to love my God, my wife, my son, my life. Forgiveness empowers you when you feel powerless because you make the choice to love or hate. James had been going on with his day-to-day life as if nothing happened, as if he had no remorse. He really seemed to care less, and even though I was in a difficult place in my life, I had to let him go.

The person who has wronged you can often really care less about you or the situation; you just go ahead with your life and do not allow that person or anyone else to hurt you in that way. I now realize that forgiveness doesn't mean that you develop brain damage, meaning you don't forget. However, just because those memories are there, don't dwell on them. They are simply that—memories.

Chapter 9

ASPIRE FOR GREATNESS

There are many people I thought of while writing this book. I thought of their individual lives and the contributions they made because they realized the purpose of their lives and the area in which they were gifted. They cultivated it to success and hung in there and kept moving no matter what, even giving their lives for that which they felt was worth believing in and striving for until excellence was achieved. Some of the more well-known include, but are not limited to, our founding father, George Washington; the father of the civil rights movement, Rev. Dr. Martin Luther King; and here recently, President Barack Obama. I had the pleasure of getting to really study President Obama, who is to me a phenomenal man. While he was on the campaign trail, I had the opportunity to read about his life and to really find out who he is—his stands on life and his beliefs—and though I do not agree with them all, I can't help but think, what if Barack Obama didn't vow to survive in all that he is supposed to be? We would have missed out on not only what he is and will mean to this country, but also the lives he was destined to bring forth. This man is not only our first black president but an inspiration to people in this country and around the world and, more personally, black men the world around. Every negative media image and stereotype was challenged when this man stood and dared to be different. His very existence and what he has accomplished confirms in me that you have to believe and work hard when there is something you want. How ironic it is that a country that once enslaved black people is now being led by a black person. Striving toward excellence is by far one thing that I believe is indestructible when coupled with a desire to believe.

One thing I feel have in common with Mr. Obama is a wife who believes in him and backs him 100 percent, and if she doesn't, she seems to have the elegance and grace to publicly not let it be known. The power that she possesses by loving him is beautiful. All that he is, is shared by her. What a beautiful sentiment to be marveled.

When you believe in yourself and have someone to share that same belief with, you feel unstoppable. Even if you are all alone, the belief in yourself can take you from feelings of worthlessness to conquering your world. Understand that you were created to excel. If you don't fulfill that which your life was created for, the void could be felt by all humanity. Something as simple as the smiles you are to cause one to have as well as the seriousness of the lives you are supposed to change and the happiness you are supposed to bring to the most important person, which is yourself just by being you. You have to be the best you that you can be and understand that the way you work through adversity can destroy or enhance the true essence of you. I had to make it so that I could encourage the lives of so many others with my own.

We overcome by the words of our testimonies. How can anyone know they are not alone if you don't tell them? Let your example be the loudest thing you say. What you do always speaks mounds above what you say, but when your words are backed up by your actions, what you have to say and the message you are relaying is magnified that much more or distorted by hypocrisy. Don't take ownership of catastrophe. Watch what you say. Words are powerful. The things we say often are not dealt with the sincerity or power of their existence. The old clichés, like your words "coming back to haunt you" or having to "eat your words" aren't just empty quotes. Your words can literally make or break the situation.

I always have had something to say, be it profound or so ridiculously funny that you would grab your stomach and double over with laughter. If I developed a saying that would get any type of response, I kept it and always said it because it got a reaction. Right before this happened to me, I found myself saying something, and up until now, the words that I uttered have haunted me because I now understand the power of the things we say. Often times when someone was tired and I'd say, "Walking is overrated unless you're in a wheelchair" seemingly those words taunt me. I'm not saying that because I said those words that is the reason this happened, but those words really explain my situation. All my life I have been told to watch what I say and even what the Bible says about putting words into the atmosphere. Seemingly the negative things that are said have more credence than the positive. I now see it has nothing to do with the sincerity of what is said. Perhaps this is caused by the lackadaisical attitude we have when we say things negatively or the lack of belief and action put forth behind the positive words.

Every new year, resolutions are made to express how the year is going to be different; we make all types of resolutions and promises, and we mean well, but life tends to obscure our beliefs, and the words that we once spoke with such fervency are met with the oppositions of life and the untamed conundrums and habits that weren't conquered the previous 365 days. Even though the words we spoke may or may not have come to pass, we have to consider the source of our request and understand the condition of our lives and the possible repercussions of receiving what we have asked for.

Chapter 10

SICKNESS AND SALVATION

I was raised in the Pentecostal church; we do all of that hand clapping and foot stomping and tongue talking and dancing in the spirit. I have seen and done some pretty amazing things. Though a lot of the rules and doctrines of the denomination that I was a part of to me are antiquated and seemingly sexist and the result of ill-interpreted Bible Scripture, the services that are held on Sundays or in a revival meeting are something that should be experienced by all. My faith in God was cultivated and developed at an early age based on the things that I would hear my mother pray for and come to pass, the Bible stories I was told in Sunday school, and hearing how God worked a miracle and healed someone or a situation was turned around in the nick of time and a catastrophic event was halted. We heard some of the greatest stories and testimonies in testimony service. We were told to just pray, and God will do anything you want and give you anything that you need. I was never really told that there is far more to it than just asking. It's complicated, especially if you are impatient or selfishly asking. God is not a sugar daddy giving you everything you want when you want and how you want. Like the old saying goes, everything good to you ain't good for you. We often quote the Scriptures that would require God to move based on the words in the Scripture, but often forget or don't quote the Scriptures in the same Bible that are non instant gratification Scriptures. It's not that the Bible is lying or in some way contradicting itself; some things in life aren't answered in the way we feel that they should be, and seeing as heaven doesn't have a customer service phone number, we must trust that the same God that created the heavens and the earth is fully capable and concerned about everything that we go through.

When I was first shot and paralyzed, I lay in bed and prayed often for God to heal me. All I could see was that I was paralyzed and couldn't walk, and I wanted God to heal me so I could get up fully healed and go on with my life. There is a bigger picture to this situation. So many things have happened; so many lives have been touched because of this situation. Some people go through things and say, "If I could do it all over again, I would do it." Not so for me, and it really takes a person being honest with themselves to say that. It is only when I think of the wonderful things that are going to come of this do I even faintly consider it. Sometimes you do have to take one for the team. Often one must go through something for the betterment of mankind or to help someone else who does not know how to overcome a bad situation.

Sometimes knowing that you are not alone and someone is going through or has gone through a situation exactly like yours, or close to it, that the words they speak or the actions of that person are encouraging and let you know that you can make it. I was often upset with God, or so I thought, because he allowed this to happen to me. I never knew that because of this my marriage would get stronger because we had nothing to fall back on except for our love for one another. I would have a chance not only to bond with my son but establish a relationship with my son. I found out who my real friends were and learned the difference between my friends and my acquaintances. I have learned how to be humble. There are some things I went through that I thought were emasculating, never thinking that I should be thankful that there was someone there to do these things for me.

One example is bedsores. If I got bedsores on my legs or back, I would have them treated, but when I got bedsores on my behind I wouldn't let my nurses know about them because I didn't want to deal with the shame or embarrassment of having them treated, not realizing that they could become infected and I could die. We sometimes pray for things when God has already made the provision. I have met some really great people who are living with paralysis, and I have learned of so many programs and organizations that exist to assist with the betterment of your quality of life. Not to mention I am now writing books that will help so many know that they are not alone and this is not the end.

I felt like God owed it to me to heal me and he should do it at once. The Bible says it. I got desperate. I named it and claimed it. I gave offerings as if I could buy a miracle. I sent off for prayer cloths and special healing waters, soaps, and bread; and still nothing happened. I grew so impatient, never stopping to ask the Lord what is was that he wanted me to learn from my situation and who my testimony going to reach? We must wait patiently on the Lord and diligently seek him. He has turned a horrible situation around and used it for my good. Sure, there are things that I have gone through that I feel are unnecessary and pointless by my standards and reasoning; but when I think of the grander scale and scope of things, I am able to say, "Not my will but thine be done." It takes trust.

That is so much easier said than done. It can be hard to follow blindly when we are concerned with life's basic necessities being taken care of, not to mention your life, which means so much to you. Trusting someone who you have never seen sounds crazy, but when you finally come to the knowledge that God has a plan for your life, it can be easier. When you can look at the promises of God instead of the situation and believe that he loves you and wants the best for you and you patiently wait on him, it always pays off. The moment you are brought out of the situation, you'll see that he was there all the time. Situations look the worst right before they come to an end. If he is your father, allow him to be your father.

You may not get all that you want right now. People pray for money all the time, wanting to be millionaires and not even being able to manage the money that they have now. If God were to bless them with millions, it may cause that person more problems than it is worth. If

God had healed me when I first asked him to, I would have continued on with life as I was used to. I would have gone back to my dead-end job, living in my one-bedroom apartment, never crossing paths with the knowledge I have attained. My life has taken such a different path than the one I planned for myself. I am not using God as a crutch. I am simply acknowledging his place in my life and finally submitting to the position I placed him in. When we give our lives to Christ, we often think that we are exempt from the perils of this life. No one ever told me of all the things I would go through or encounter; all that I was told is Jesus loves you and he wants to give you the desires of your heart. Whenever you pray, he will answer. I thought it was a pretty sweet deal, not knowing what was going to be required of me. God showed his love for us by sending his son, Jesus, to die on the cross for our sins. We show our love for him by giving over complete control to him and living a life that pleases him.

Some may argue that if God really loved me, he wouldn't have let me get shot—all they're seeing is the negative, not realizing that my very life was spared. Had I not been like this, I would not have been able to do things as I now do. My life now has purpose and a clear destiny all because I was shot.

I don't want to go through this. Even Jesus prayed for a way of escape when he was to be crucified. The flesh doesn't like pain or uncomfortable situations. At the end of his prayer, he said, "Not my will but thy will be done." At that point, he surrendered his will and fully trusted his father. It seemed so pointless for him to die like he did, but at that time there was no remission for sin without the shedding of innocent blood. He couldn't have just had a heart attack and died; he had to be beaten up, and the Bible tells us that by his stripes we are healed. Each event had a purpose, and even though it seems morbid and unnecessary, we don't understand fully the mind of God or why he does the things he does. The trials and tribulations we go through in life aren't just bad things happening to good people. They have purpose.

When a child asks a parent for some candy and they say no, the reason doesn't matter to that child or even make sense—all they can see is "I want this candy." The child's parent could be saying no for a whole host of reasons. It could be that if the child eats the candy, it will spoil their appetite for an upcoming meal that their body needs for nourishment or because sugar can rot the teeth and the parent doesn't want the child's teeth to rot. Or the fact that too much candy can make you sick or maybe it's a no for right now, but instead of the child thinking, "My parents know what is best for me and they are protecting me from unseen dangers because they love me," all that child sees is that "My parents said no and I want it." A delay doesn't mean a denial; there are some things that we may not get, and it's for our own good.

So many people have acquired so much stuff, money, clothes, cars, jewelry. So much time is spent buying more and maintaining their possessions that they take no thought for their soul. When this earthly vessel that we live in dies, where will we go? Understand that this body is no more the true you than a glove is your hand. Treasure stored on Earth, no matter how wonderful they are, can in no way compare to treasure you give by sharing yourself and experiences with another to help them.

Love is the greatest commandment; if mankind could love each other as we love ourselves, all of the world's problems would be solved; there would be no hunger because we would make sure our fellow man had food before we fed ourselves. No war, no homelessness. We can become so caught up with our own agendas that we forget about others. Once you truly yield yourself to God and his purpose for your life, you will then see your life has to do more than about only you. Just because you give your life to God, you are not granted instant immunity from life's trials and tribulations; it means that you have a power working in you to turn situations that are heading one way completely around. Help in the times of trouble. At some point in our lives, we will face situations that are seemingly insurmountable. Some catastrophic event befalls our lives or the life of a loved one … something that is unable to be fixed by your own power. Money can't do it, doctors can't fix it, nor can your loved ones wish it away. That's seemingly the time we turn to God. We should turn to God in every situation. He is the only one who can truly fix any situation or has the power to sustain you until the appointed time has come for your deliverance of whatever the problem is you are facing.

The only way to give a problem to God is with no strings attached to it. Meaning that if God doesn't move the way you want him to or when you want him to, you will not try and fix it yourself. A person can have a terminal illness and go on through life unaffected until they find out that they have the disease, and then they are dead in a week. You have to make a decision as to whose report you will believe. I'm not saying not to get treatment for the ailment; what I am saying is even though you are told it is one way, believe that God can heal you. I believe that God is going to heal me from paralysis. Point blank, I refuse to believe that I am going to remain the way I am right now. I rest in the fact that even though I am often hospitalized due to complications from this infirmity, if I take my focus off of what I was promised by God, I will surely die. My faith has been tried and tested to the point where I felt like giving up and allowing whatever was going to happen to happen. I have been praying for years to be healed, and my world was shaken at its very foundation when I had to have my leg amputated. Giving up at this point seemed logical. How I could ever walk again? I only have one leg! I didn't realize that people walk on prostheses all the time. All the stops had been placed in my path that would make me focus on the creation rather than the creator.

While we wait, we must occupy our time wisely and, as odd as it may seem, prepare for that which you desire from God. I have always been big. I was skinny as a kid, but in junior high school, I ballooned to two hundred pounds. In my adult life, my heaviest was 406 pounds. So I am changing my eating habits not only to be healthier but to get the excess weight off so that I can avoid the complications I may face walking on a prosthetic leg. Faith without work is dead; we have to put forth an effort in order to receive. Do all you can and diligently take care of what you have now. I have seen God do the impossible. Don't panic about bad news; realize that nothing catches God off guard or surprises him.

There are some things we pray for that only requires being a good steward to attain. For instance, a new car or house—well, if we pay our bills on time and maintain good credit we can have those things. We don't have to rely on a miracle because our credit is too bad for us to get it on our own. Often we need to prove we really want what we are asking for by making the provision for it before it is tangible.

A couple who is going to have a baby will often turn a room in their house into a nursery. They may buy a crib and clothes and stuffed animals for the coming baby. They don't have the baby in their hands, but because the woman is pregnant and won't stay that way forever, they know that a baby is coming. That is the same way our faith in God needs to be in order to get results. We don't have it in our hands yet. I am so convinced it is going to happen because God said it would; and when it comes, I will be as prepared as I can to receive it. And if for some reason it is delayed, I won't doubt it is going to happen.

We must also live a life that pleases God. Being a good person isn't enough. God must be placed as priority one in our lives—above our children, our spouses, family, friends, our jobs, hobbies, and even ourselves. Time should be spent daily reading our Bible and praying. Without faith it is impossible to please God. How can you learn about him without spending time with him?

I am not handy by any definition when it comes to using written directions to assemble something. If I were to buy something that needed assembly, I would be totally at a loss, but if I read the instructions patiently and closely follow the directions, I could do it. If I needed help I'd call on my older brother for help. The same goes for life: if we follow the commandments of God and call on God or, if need be, our brother or sister (both biological and through friendship) to help us when we are in need, success is inevitable. We can do all things through Christ, who strengthens us. Believe that he can and will supply all of your needs and the desires of your heart. Don't panic or give up when things are hard. The creator creates solutions all the time.

Chapter 11

ANOTHER CHAPTER

Just when I thought things were looking up, I was faced with yet another great challenge. My wife became ill, and this proved to be a very challenging and eye-opening experience.

My wife and I sometimes argue. Just as in any relationship, you will not always see eye to eye, but when it happens between us, I often just remain quiet until it blows over, often forgetting the reason for the altercation that at the time seemed so major.

As humans we have egos and want to be right, so much so that truth and resolution are often reduced in importance. This particular incident took a turn one winter evening in November. We had been arguing earlier that day on into the evening. My wife was in our kitchen, cutting up vegetables so that I could cook dinner; this is something that she always does. Even in anger you cannot forget who you are or allow your anger for that person or situation to be foolishly retaliated by actions that make you act out of character. My wife and I act as a team to get things done in our household and our lives. I only have full function in one hand, and when we prepare our meals, she cuts up things like fruit and vegetables. I can still cook the meals, but using a knife is a bit unsafe—that's just the way that we have worked this out.

This particular night my wife and I had a pretty heated argument. It was close to dinner time, and I needed to get dinner ready and I needed her help. She could have said, "I'm mad, and I'm not cutting up anything!" which would have been retaliation against me because she knows how much I love cooking. I could have retaliated against her by saying, "I'm not cooking," because I know how much she loves my cooking. Had that happened, we would have both had to go to bed hungry, and by trying to spite each other, we really would end up causing a bigger problem for ourselves.

Meanwhile, while she was chopping up vegetables, she began to feel very strange. Strange things began to go on in her body, and that's when she broke the monotonous silence by saying, "When I'm finished chopping up these vegetables, I'm going to the hospital." When she said this to me, I immediately stopped our childish game of silent treatment, and it is at this point that resolution needed to take its rightful place. My wife hates the hospital, and for her to utter those words were simply frightening to me. She said she was going numb in different areas of her body. The reason that this was so frightening to her was because of her mother. She remembered that her mother was so young when she began to have strokes in her brain, and numbness is one of the major symptoms. I immediately dialed 911. When the paramedics arrived, they immediately rushed her to the hospital. When all of the excitement was over, my son and I looked at each other, neither of us knowing what to do. We knew that we had to go to the hospital, but how? She was the one who did all the driving. In that moment I realized just how much my wife meant in our lives. We were literally stuck without her. I realized then my wife was the one who campaigned most for my quality of life. My life often is difficult; I don't even want to imagine what my life would be like without her.

My wife was in the hospital for about five days, and the only medical diagnosis that was given was, "Something is going on in your body that is causing you to be ill. However, we don't know what it is." To make matters worse, her health insurance would not allow her to be in the hospital any longer because the doctors could not substantiate a strong enough case for her to be there; after all, they had no idea what was wrong with her. So she now had to check out of the hospital and go home and wait to be seen by a neurologist. By doctors' orders, due to the condition of her health, she was told not to return to work or drive until they found out what was going on, a definite diagnosis was attained, she began treatment for whatever was found, and her symptoms no longer persisted. This would prove to have a major effect on our family, primarily because the majority of running the household and seeing after my wife and our son were now completely my responsibility. Financially, it was be difficult because she was not working and bringing in a paycheck, and our bills are satisfied by both our incomes. To top it off, we were approaching the beginning of the holiday season, just one week before Thanksgiving, and this year we really wanted our son to have a lot to open for Christmas and be able to get each other something nice. After all, this was finally a holiday season when I was not sick or in the hospital. I know that giving gifts is not the major focal point or the reason for celebration; this would be one of the first Christmases in our home together as a family.

After my wife was finally seen by the neurologist, she was sent on test after grueling test. I remember being so angry because I felt like some of the tests were so unnecessary, not to mention extremely painful, and as with the doctors, the neurologist didn't find anything either, though he could visibly see that something was wrong. I did my best to care for my wife, son, and our household. I must say that I gained a new respect for my wife and people all over the world who run households and care for children. It was not hard because I am in a wheelchair; it is just hard.

The human body has a funny way of healing itself. With much prayer and after time, my wife gradually began to get better. Currently she is undergoing tests to find the reason why she experiences bouts of vertigo, sporadic numbness, and extreme weakness in her extremities at the least amount of physical exertion. But it worked out in our favor because she had not been released back to work, and right at the same time that she started feeling better, I was back in the hospital, and it would have been havoc for her to find a sitter for our son every day while she went to work and tried to visit me in the hospital.

Normally on holidays, we spend time at each of our parents' homes, and if we have time, we go by a few friends' homes. This year both our parents were not sure what their plans were going to be, so we agreed to do Thanksgiving dinner with my best friend and her family and go to both of our parents' homes and spend time with them. However, after the doctor's order that my wife could not drive, those plans were halted. My wife's boss knew her situation and purchased us a complete Thanksgiving turkey dinner with all the trimmings. We were so thankful for her foresight and compassion. None of our family or friends, with the exception of our pastor, stopped by that day to say hi or anything. This really upset the both of us because everyone knew of our situation, and it really seemed as if they didn't care. It is almost pointless becoming angry with people for not reacting to your situation in the way you think or expect they should or with what you feel would be a satisfactory reaction. You will find yourself having fewer arguments and family feuds—even if something is done to you that you wouldn't dare do to another—when you accept the fact that people are who they are and you have to let them be themselves.

We came to the end of yet another day, and this night I decided to sleep in the bed. I had been sleeping in my wheelchair just in case my wife needed something in the middle of the night. I was acting as a nurse instead of a patient, and it was a major transition; however, it would not last until I nursed her back to health. When I arose the next morning, I was in pain like I have never experienced. I knew something was wrong, but I tried to dismiss it. I took some pain medication, thinking I would soon feel better, but after lying there for two hours, I didn't get any relief. I felt like it might be a severe urinary tract infection, which I had often experienced but never with shortness of breath. I thought that was quite odd so I called my doctor for another dose of antibiotics. However, as I lay there, my condition worsened. My wife called 911. When the paramedics arrived, I looked over at my son and gave him an all-too-often-recited speech that Daddy was okay and that I was just going to the hospital to get some medicine to ease his mind.

Ritualistically, I was hooked up to the paramedics' monitors to see the state of my vital signs, and oddly enough everything was fine. But I didn't have the peace of mind from knowing everything was fine. When the paramedics asked me if I still wanted to go to the hospital, I reluctantly said no; after all, my vital signs were fine. They radioed ahead and canceled the ambulance that was on the way to my home to transport me to the hospital, but much to my surprise, they arrived anyway. Oddly enough, they never got the call. I took this as a sign that I really needed to go and be seen about. When I was placed on the gurney and into the ambulance, I was hooked up to their equipment, and it showed very different information. The concern shifted from a urinary tract infection to a now possible heart attack. I was not even that scared. I guess because there was so much I had been through so far. As I lay there on the gurney, my mind went through all I had been through over the last four years and all I had to bear, and tears couldn't even roll because I was tired. Not so much physically but mentally, spiritually, and emotionally.

I thought of how my home had been invaded and how I had been shot as a result of this invasion. I was paralyzed. When I was in the hospital because of this gunshot, my brother had my car and was at the right place at the wrong time, and it was shot while it was parked outside of a friend's house when their neighbors began to feud. The hospital negligently caused bedsores to plague my body, which would later go on to threaten my life. I missed the birth of my son, my firstborn child. I lost my best friend; my wife had no steady place to lay her head on while she was carrying my child. Friends turned their backs on me. I have constantly done stints in the hospital that would last months at a time. We have been homeless, and now I lay there with oxygen being pumped into my nose, not even having enough strength in my body to sit up due to the weakness in my arms compounded with the news of an MRI that said I now have multiple sclerosis.

There was so much more going through my mind, and that's when I began to pray. "Lord, I'm tired, but please don't let me die." Even in the back of my mind, I was thinking death would be such a sweet release, but I didn't want to make my wife a widow or have my son call another man "Dad."

When we arrived at the hospital, the staff was awaiting my arrival. After much testing, they found that, thankfully, I had not had a heart attack. It was discovered that I had a horrible infection in the wounds on my body. The doctors began to administer heavy doses of intravenous antibiotics, and within hours, my temperature went from 102 degrees to normal. I thought that everything would be fine and I could finish the antibiotics at home. To my surprise, the doctors informed me I would need to undergo a blood transfusion, so I had to be admitted to the hospital. I grew to hate those words but I complied. When I received the first of three pints of blood, my body did not accept it, and I began to have a terrible reaction. My heart began to race, I was sweating profusely, and my temperature shot up to 103. The nurse immediately stopped the blood transfusion and administered medicine to counteract the side effects that I was having. I later was told that had the transfusion continued, I would have died. I was in the hospital for about eight days, and my condition seemed to be improving, so I was sent home. We ended up having to spend yet another Christmas in the hospital, but it was fine; we were used to it and so thankful I was still alive. I was released from the hospital New Year's Eve 2008. My family and I went home, and because it was late, we just watched the ball drop in Times Square and the fireworks show here in Las Vegas and we went to sleep.

New Year's Day, I woke up feeling just fine; however, later on that night I started feeling the same way I did the morning I originally went to the hospital. We called the ambulance, and I went back to the hospital. This time it was different. I really felt like this time I was going in to take care of business and not just be treated and released or pumped full of pills. There was an "enough is enough" feeling I kept having. I would later see that feeling was truly warranted.

After extensive testing and many needle pokes, we found that the infection was coming from a wound on my left ankle. When I was shot, I was leaning against our bedroom door to make it hard for the intruders to gain access. When they shot through our bedroom door, the bullet severed my spinal cord. I could no longer stand up, and I fell onto the floor behind my bedroom door, and the police had to kick in my door in order to get me out. I don't know if it happened when I fell or when the door was kicked in, but my ankle and leg were broken; my leg healed, but my ankle never did. The doctors told me not to worry about it because I was not walking anyway, and if I ever did start back walking, they would just fuse everything together. So my ankle was broken for nearly five years; my foot could literally touch the side of my leg. I developed a wound where the ankle fracture was. The wound started on one side of my ankle and ran clear through to the other side on the opposite side of my foot. The infection had now infected my bone, and I once again developed osteomyelitis.

After weeks of antibiotics, the infection was showing no signs up clearing up and was now in my bloodstream. The doctor said we had to act fast, and I had no other option but amputation. Doctors had suggested that to me years ago and I wouldn't accept it. I got six different medical opinions, and they all said the same thing. I was desperately seeking an alternative. I was devastated. I had prayed so many times. *God, please heal these wounds.* I remember praying to wake up one day with all the wounds gone. I was tired of all the dressing changes, the foul odors, and the wounds draining through the bandages and onto my clothes. When I first came home from the hospital, I didn't know that with a spinal cord injury your body has trouble regulating temperature. It could be freezing cold outside and I could be burning up hot—or scorching hot outside and I'd be freezing cold. One summer day in August I was freezing cold and couldn't warm up. My wife gave me about six blankets and opened up our bedroom window so the heat could come in, but nothing worked. I turned on a space heater, and it was helping some but not enough, so in desperation I put the heater under the covers with me and it finally warmed me up. So when I was finally warm, I pulled the covers back and looked at my legs. I was horrified. I had literally cooked my left leg. I had third-degree burns from my behind down to my calf. The heat burned my leg, and I didn't feel a thing. The burn was so bad that four and half years later it was still not completely healed.

This is the same leg that they said I would have to have amputated. I was told it was going to be amputated at my calf. One of the doctors on my case advised me that this was no longer my decision. "What do you mean?" I replied. He said, "At this point it is no longer about you. You have to consider your wife and child."

I was in a very fragile state. I was risking dying from the infection that was now in my bloodstream because once your blood is infected, it spreads to all of your organs, and death is almost inevitable. This is a prime example of what I stated in this book a few chapters ago, that you will be surprised to know how little your life has to do about you.

The physician explained to me that if I were young and single, I could take my chances. "However, you have a family depending on you." He said that he would send a surgeon in to talk to me and explain all that I would need to know and discuss any possible options I had. To my misfortune, the surgeon agreed that an amputation would be the only way to go at this time, and it would have to be higher than what I was told because of the burn on my leg. The open tissue ran the risk of becoming infected. I don't know what it is about those few inches, but I just lost it emotionally. I guess I just was not ready to hear that. I had time to prepare mentally for the below-the-knee amputation, but this was something totally new and different.

I had only three days before they wanted to operate. That night I turned off all my phones and the television and asked the nurse to close the door. This was a major life-changing decision ahead of me, so I knew I had to pray. I prayed for hours, asking God for a sign that this was what I needed to do. Do I go ahead with the surgery or not? While lying there in my hospital bed praying, I envisioned three huge letters lit up like a neon sign. YES. I felt a peace like I had never felt before, and after that I then knew what I had to do.

It took me two days after my surgery to build up enough courage to look at my leg, and when I did, it hurt me to my very core. I couldn't even comprehend what I was looking at. My wife, by my side as always, grabbed my hand; and in silence I cried. This was harder to me than when I lay on my bedroom floor paralyzed. When I was paralyzed, I was drugged very heavily, and I never knew what was really going on, and when I was finally sober and cognitive enough to know what was up, I never accepted it for myself. This amputation was permanent, however. I resolved to this one fact: either I will miraculously grow another leg or I will have to go and buy one, but one day by faith I will get up, turn around, and look at this wheelchair, new leg and all, and with a smile on my face and praise on my lips I will walk again.

Don't ever allow the dream inside you to die because you feel that an obstacle you face is too tumultuous or so overwhelming that you miscarry due to being lax and plagued with procrastination. Life and mankind need you. Don't worry about the impact you will have because you may never know just who needs it. The one who may need it most could very well be you.

Chapter 12

LET YOUR FAITH BE THE AUTHOR OF YOUR DREAMS

In my experience, my reality has been challenged by being paralyzed, having limits placed on my life, and having the things I did for enjoyment in life be stifled. By that I mean the way that I thought life was and my perception of people and their reactions to situations—life as I knew it prior to this. I also have a different understanding of dreams and of faith. I now see that without faith, dreams are powerless.

As a child I remember my parents always telling me how smart I was and that I could do or be anything. They said this based on what they saw in me, and even though they could see or dream, if you will, what was on the inside of me, I did not have the faith within myself to grab hold of what they were seeing in me. I didn't view myself as this intelligent child, and this was often said to me when I was being reprimanded after doing something that wasn't too intelligent. My parents realized how intelligent I was and had trouble understanding why I didn't use better reasoning and decision-making skills.

Greatness is in me, but it wasn't until I came into the knowledge that I could begin to utilize it. I can have a dream, and that dream can be wonderful. It could be a dream that would be financially self-sustaining or the answer to great health. It is not until I begin to truly believe that it is more than a possibility; rather, now it is in my mind a reality. No longer is my dream an unattainable hope. I believe in it so strongly that I have begun to mentally see the environment around it. A vernacular for its existence is produced, not based on anything else, but I can do this.

It is as if my dream has become impregnated by my faith. I like the example in the Bible that faith without work is dead. Meaning, until you begin to work toward cultivating your dream or reality, faith, no matter how great, is useless. A formula that I have begun to work on is dreams + faith + work = success.

There is no quick fix for earned greatness. I have sat and listened to so many people talk about their dreams and what they would like to do or what they are good at and how they would love to be rich and what things they will acquire if it were to happen. The conversation is great, and after a while, somehow the dream turns into nothing more than a story that is so often repeated. It has lost its value even to the bearer of the story—oftentimes because more effort has gone into telling the dream rather than working for that which is desired.

I have had to allow myself to pair my faith with prayer as my work for the final part of the success equation as it pertains to my life. Oftentimes the reality of your dream can only be achieved through divine intervention. I want to walk again. I know that my body wants to because it was created to do that and it did. However, there are currently no means by which this is humanly tangible. So I am working by doing what the Bible tells us to do in order to receive what is not in man's power to grant.

Understand that the trying of your faith creates patience, and by that you will appreciate what you have dreamed and are now working for. People often want to help people in need before finding out the true need or if there is one. If I had a penny for every time someone has told me to keep the faith, I would be quite wealthy by now. My frustration has never been with my faith not being strong but rather with patience. When I asked God to heal me, I believed he would, and

I have stood, theoretically speaking of course. My frustration has not been "Can this happen?" but instead "When will this happen?"

We can so plainly see potential in others, but when it comes to ourselves, potential can often be stifled by self-perception. The way we need to view ourselves is similar to a child's view of a parent. I waited for months for my son to start talking when he was first born, and now I sometimes long for those days because he just won't stop. He asks me question upon question no matter what is going on, simply because he sees something in me. An answer. He believes that I will know what he doesn't simply because of who I am.

Everyone has someone or something that is or, at one time or another, was of great importance. When you become emotionally attached, protection becomes second nature. Like a mother with her child, protect your dream. Let no hurt, harm, or danger come to it, be it by words or actions. I was so sure that clearly everyone would want this for me just as bad as I wanted it. Not so. You hold value in something because of emotional attachment and because of how you see it based on the place it holds in your heart.

Understand that not everyone will accept your dream in their reality like you do. I once heard a story about a woman who was speaking on behalf of her son, who had raped a young lady and was now in jail. All the mother could say was, "But my son is a good boy, he's a good boy." She raised her son and knew the values she had instilled in him and loved him. However, all the victim knew was that this man was a monster. She definitely couldn't see this good boy that the mother was talking about based on her situation. People may not be in the same place that you are as far as the way you see things. It is important that you choose wisely who you discuss your dream with because not everybody will understand what you see.

Consider the Bible story of Jesus walking on water. The disciples were in a ship. They were distraught because John the Baptist had just been murdered, and though they were with Jesus, he had ventured off to a mountain, leaving the disciples in the boat. Because of strong winds the boat had drifted into the middle of the sea. Jesus saw the boat and walked on the water to the disciples. When the disciples saw

Jesus walking on the water they were afraid and wondered if this was a ghost they were seeing. Peter then said to Jesus, "If that is you, allow me to come to you," and he began to walk on the water along with Jesus. However, the wind became so rough that he lost his balance and began to sink. In fear of drowning, he called out to Jesus to save him. Of course Jesus saved him and said, "O ye of little faith." They boarded the ship and the winds ceased.

Let's walk through this story and compare it to our lives and our situations. The disciples had just received horrible news of the death of not just a friend but one of their leaders. When trouble strikes, it always seems to be a worst-case scenario and often something that shakes you to your very core.

Trouble never travels alone. Even when the disciples were in the presence of Jesus, he left and their boat drifted out to sea, and Jesus, who could help them, was nowhere in sight. Oftentimes when we face trouble, it can feel as though no one is there, not even God. Peter, seeing Jesus, though he was scared, saw a glimmer of hope and said, "If that is you, let me come to you." When we have faith, it has to override fear. Faith and fear are like oil and water; they do not mix. Our faith can be strong. Peter had a vision or a dream, if you will, that mustered up his faith; and he took that step and began to walk on the water. We often start off so strong, giving something all that we have. When the wind made Peter lose his balance, he began to sink. I compare this to hitting bumps in the road on the way to what we want—trials and tribulations. Had Peter kept his focus on what he wanted and where he was going afterward as opposed to what things looked liked, he would have been fine. It is not easy to keep faith strong when trouble comes, but it is necessary that we don't lose sight of what we are wanting and believing can happen.

When Peter began to sink, he cried out for Jesus to save him, and the Bible says Jesus stretched his hand out and saved him. This has two meanings. One is that when things look bad, though we have lost sight of our goal and began to fail, we can call out to God to help us; and even if we have messed up, God will still not only be there with us but will also help us out and come to our rescue. Secondly, the Bible says Jesus stretched out his hand and saved Peter. Peter's dream or goal was not to walk on water; he only wanted to come to Jesus. It was Jesus who gave the pathway of walking on the water. Our road to where we want to be can seem so unnecessary and impossible. It can seem like you must walk on water to get what you want. Understand that Peter did not know how he was going to get to Jesus, and he was not even sure that he was looking at Jesus, but his faith was strong enough to know that if it was Jesus, he would make a way for him to come to him. Next we see that Peter was only an arm's length away from Jesus when he began to sink. We can give up too soon. Oftentimes right before we are closest to the finish line, things get the hardest. That is why it is so important that we don't give up on what we want and are working for, no matter what things look like. Jesus then said, "O ye of little faith." It was no one's fault Peter failed but his own. As soon as they boarded the ship, the weather became calm.

The Bible doesn't say it, but my own failures and my imagination can give me some insight as to how Peter must have felt. He was so close to having what he wanted. I can imagine he beat himself up mentally pretty bad. We can beat ourselves up to the point of death, or we can use it as a stepping stone and lessons well learned to never repeat the same mistake again and, most importantly, realize that God is there to bring us out of trouble safely even when we cause the failure, no matter how bad it is.

This way of thinking, believing and living it has helped me remain so positive through my walking-on-water situation. If I consider my windy moments, much like Peter, I, too, will fail. To avoid disappointment and fantasy, I have found it best not to dream further than faith and work ethic can take me. It is in us as people to defy odds and strive for greatness because we were created in the image of greatness.

Failure must be granted permission in order to exist.

Miscarriage is termed that way in this chapter to give substance or a definition to the loss of a dream, hope, or vision; it is just that, the misappropriation of something due to circumstances beyond your control. Situations and circumstances can impede you from bringing forth that idea, vision, dream, or life that you desire. When something is beyond your control, you must rely on one who supersedes your ability to change that which is beyond your power. You must believe that there are forces working beyond your control that have an impact on your life. If for no other reason you believe this, consider your birth. You had very little to do with your conception. Our lives are complicated; it would take an individual fluent in all manner of thinking to fully comprehend the obvious reasons of outcomes, not to mention the hidden reasons not seen. There are situations and circumstances that go on in our individual lives that we have no control over, no matter how we plan and prepare for them. If it is not for us to be in that realm we are going after, opposition is inevitable.

For example, a person may desire to become a fireman; perhaps their father and grandfather were firemen, and they want to follow in their footsteps. As a child the gifts they played with or received were all based on fireman like attributes. Their gifts may have been fire engines, ladders, play water hoses, etc. I mean, it was really supposed to happen. It was a given. Not much thought was ever given to any other profession because this person just knew that they were supposed to become a fireman.

Suppose one day while on a family skiing vacation, this aspiring fireman is flying down snow-covered slopes, the crisp wind blowing in his face, and he is having the time of his life. Then all of a sudden he sees a tree directly in his path. He zigzags but can't avoid slamming into the tree. He was doing about twenty-five miles per hour, and despite all his efforts and training, *boom*, he hits the tree. The impact immediately renders him unconscious, and when this person regains consciousness, he tries to get up on his feet. Despite all his efforts he cannot move his legs. Confused, he reaches down to see why he can't stand up and soon realizes that he can't feel his legs. Panicking, he goes into shock, and being paralyzed terrifies his mind. After being rushed to a hospital and after extensive testing, the doctor delivers the earth-shattering news that he will never walk again. After he has processed the mind-blowing news, he realizes that all of his dreams and preparations for ever becoming a fireman are now over. There is no way that it would ever be an option for him. This person no longer possesses the physical skills required to operate in this profession. The dream to operate in this particular realm is over, and never again will that be an option. This dream was not given up voluntarily, however, even though his dreams of becoming a firefighter are over and he thinks, "Those were the plans that were set up for my life."

That person may not be able to run into a burning building to save a life or even use the Jaws of Life to cut the mangled steel of an automobile to free the victim of a car accident, and how are they to operate in a totally different realm now? By their testimony. For someone who has given up hope in their situation, hearing what you have gone through and how you made it out can literally give one the hope they need to live. This person can still save lives.

Despite the often tragic and confusing complications that come along with a miscarriage, as long as the womb—or mind, if you will—is still functional, the conception and rebirth of a dream is still attainable, though it is now different. Though this may seem tragic, it could really be the best thing that could ever happen to you.

When I was a child I wanted to be a fireman. No other family members were in that profession or anything close to that field. Though the injury I sustained was not from skiing, nevertheless it was a life-changing injury. This was something personal that I always wanted. It was not until high school, when I entered and performed in a talent show doing standup comedy, that this was altered. My sights changed, so I began to work toward this dream of being a famous standup comedian. I wrote jokes in my joke book constantly; I would always practice my jokes. Oftentimes if I wanted to try a new joke out, I would somehow work it into a conversation to see if the person I was talking to would laugh. They may have thought it was conversation, but in actuality, I was trying a joke out on them to see if it was funny before I took it out on stage. I would perform sometimes for free (mostly for church folks). However, I didn't care because I loved comedy; for me there is no better feeling than ending a set where you have just worked the crowd over.

Though I haven't yet attained national popularity, I'm pretty well-known in the church community here in Las Vegas, the audience I was going after anyway. This is one of the things that I was created to do. There have been things I needed to do to sustain myself when I was not performing or the money was not coming in, but I never have lost sight of what it is that I am here for and what brings me and countless others joy. When I got shot, I just knew my dreams of a successful comedy career were over. *I'm paralyzed, how can I do standup?* I couldn't even stand up, and my comedy was always very physical. So one day at a birthday party for my pastor's wife I performed from my chair, and even though I couldn't bounce around on stage like I used to, I was still funny.

You have to pray and look deep within yourself to find ways to operate in opposition and to live the life that you know is yours—your reason for living. I may not be saving lives the same way firefighters do, but now I am uplifting hearts when I do comedy, and that in a sense is a lifesaver. We were placed on this earth to accomplish a certain number of things, reach a certain number of people, and experience personal pleasures and pain; and in some ways, doing those things, to me, means a truly fulfilled and successful life. Making tons of money in life might make you think you are happy, but do you have joy? Joy comes from God because it is not predicated wonderful. That's why when you are doing what you are truly called to do, though you may become agitated from the lack of cooperation from others or the long hours and short pay, you continue to do it with a passion because it brings you joy, a sense of satisfaction that really can be in words. Frustration that brings about satisfaction isn't easy to comprehend, let alone explain to someone else. When you find what it is your life is supposed to be spent doing, do it and with all your might and without complaining.

This is your life. Part of it is a compilation of beings based on the people you have added to it, and you have got to live it that way. I always thought my mother gave too much of herself to her children, especially when they were grown and dealing with situations and circumstances that they caused for themselves, and I would often talk to my mom and be frank, telling her to get a life. Now that I look back, what I was really saying was, "Mom, don't forget about you in the process of doing so much for others." I know that we must help each other, and at times our passion to help may come at the risk of neglecting ourselves, but we cannot forget that we are also a person with thoughts, feelings, and emotions, along with a desire for ourselves to be happy.

Even though you may face opposition in doing that which you are called to do, you cannot end the course of greatness that is destined for your life because you have to achieve it in an unconventional way. And more importantly you cannot base your success on the outcomes of others who have achieved success according to them or others in a similar circumstance. When your accomplishment has been executed, when you have done what you were supposed to do, the outcome is success.

You can never be completely sure how people will react. Just do what you are supposed to do wholeheartedly. A great response would be wonderful and oftentimes it follows, but don't allow that to be your reason for doing or the measure by which you gauge your own personal success. Don't ever give up on your own life. Postponement does not mean it is over; it is merely a negotiation with time, and seeing as how none of us knows exactly how much we have, as soon as you can, grasp some sense of normalcy after a bump in the road. Go after it with all your might. It is a matter of life before your death.

On the other hand is abortion. Don't abort the dream you have inside of you, whether it is to change the world or to allow your life to change someone else's life because it would mean the world to them. People, for years, have tried to figure out the meaning of life; and that is an enormous waste of time. Our minds could not grasp it anyway. We only have theory. Who could really explain the mysteries of this life? We should fully concentrate on how we can make the most of every moment, living life to its fullest. In my short lifetime, I have had over twenty jobs, never loving or liking one of them for that matter; but when I'm on stage I'm like a fish to water. I could always go back to a nine to five, but I would never be fulfilled, and it would be just that. I've heard that "job" is the acronym for *just over broke*. Broken physically, financially, and spiritually, don't abort the dream that gives you total fulfillment in all areas. Though you may not know the reason for living, you can bask in the reason you lived.

I repeat, when you use abortion in situations, you are using Godlike power without Godlike wisdom and knowledge.

Abortion is a very powerful, self-destructive, and temporary resolution. Alleviating a problem yourself using this method gives you Godlike power without godlike wisdom. When we read in the Bible and see God exercise his power and his ability to change the course of events drastically, it was always because of disobedience against his word, not because of convenience. Abortion is a topic that I can offer up much conversation on because I have had a lot of dealings in this area. When I participated in the first abortion I must say that there was a great deal of temporary mental release for me because at seventeen years old, I didn't want to have to face the rigors or embarrassment of being a teen father. I didn't want to have to face the girl's mother, although I believe that she knew the truth all along. The repercussions have been absolutely horrible—nightmares and night sweats and even now the constant thoughts of *what if.* Every time I run into Olivia, even though we have forgiven each other, the thought of what happened in the past is always in the back of our minds. I often wonder how different my life could have been if I hadn't cheated myself of the opportunity to be a father, not to mention the mental anguish I suffered with abortions two and three. All the horrible thoughts I must now deal with could have been the wonderful memories that come with rearing children. A temporary fix has now caused a lifelong question. I see what a driving force child can be for excellence in life, and while I thought I was doing myself a favor, I really did myself an injustice. Things may have been difficult had I decided to step up, but I could have worked through it, and no one could have stopped me.

Abortion, in the sense of what I am trying to convey in this book, means not accepting what is in your life that you have been called or chosen to do. It would equate to working on a job you hate just because the money is good. You hate getting up and going, you hate it the whole time you are there, and there might even be things you must do on that job that challenge your morals. Money is wonderful and a necessity in this life and money is not evil. It is the love of money that is evil. When you begin to do things that are totally against who you are, you become a slave to money. Do not allow the fear of not having money force you into irrational decision making or aborting your dream.

I will use, for example, a very famous African American talk show hostess I really admire. I don't totally agree with certain views she has, but this woman is absolutely phenomenal. The selflessness of this individual seems to be more than admirable as well as the strides she has made to influence and improve the lives of others. She has made an awesome influence on not just her life but the lives of so many others. Suppose when her life got rough, or on the road to where she was going, she simply said, "This is too hard or too much, I give up." Every single life that her life was created to touch would not have been impacted. Not to say that their lives would not have been touched or impacted in some way by someone else, but her special touch and the unique impact she made in their lives and the self-fulfillment that she may have received by doing that would have been missed.

That is why it is so important that you be pro-life in regard to your own life. I don't mean the decision of a woman's right to choose. Don't get me wrong, that is an entirely different subject. I mean as an individual. The seeming unfairness of life has caused many to abort. Don't be so afraid of life and its uncertainty; we can become complacent in comfort ability. We need a certain amount of shaking up in our lives to go on to other things. If I had never been thrust into this situation, I would have never known about living life with challenges and how to overcome them. Neither would I have had a front-row seat in the lives of so many who are dealing with similar issues.

Take writing this book, for instance. I have never really wanted to write a book, and if it had not been for this chapter in my life, I probably never would have. When I was shot, the bullet entered my arm and caused so much damage that I really only have full function and use of one arm and hand, but I typed a book with one hand, and that gives me a sense of self-satisfaction that will be there even if I only sell one copy (which I know won't because my momma will buy one and so will my wife, so that's at least two!). Abortion is no longer an option; the sense of satisfaction you receive from running an obstacle course isn't from the obstacle—it's crossing the finish line and looking back on what you did. There is an old spiritual song that says, "My soul looks back and wonders how I got over."

My journey has not been an easy one, and it's not because I prayed so much that I got over. It's because I knew God heard me—that's what got me through. What if Mary, pregnant with Jesus, had said to her husband, Joseph, "I give up. I just can't go on. My life has taken a turn that makes things too uncomfortable for me," and aborted Jesus? What condition or outcome would the world have? Where would I be? Where would you be? Don't abort yourself.

We have to forgive. We must survive.